ANGLICAN CATHEDRALS

Aberdeen	St Andrews Cathedral	Lichfield	Cathedral Church of the Blessed Virgin Mary and St Chad
Armagh	Cathedral Church of St Patrick	Lincoln	Cathedral Church of the Blessed Virgin Mary
Bangor	Cathedral Church of St Deiniol	Lisburn	Cathedral Christ Church
Bath and Wells	Cathedral Church of St Andrew in Wells	Liverpool	Cathedral Church of Christ
Belfast	Cathedral Church of St Anne	Llandaff	Cathedral Church of SS Peter and Paul with SS Dyfrig, Teilo and Euddogwy
Birmingham	Cathedral Church of St Philip	London	Cathedral Church of St Paul
Blackburn	Cathedral Church of St Mary the Virgin	Manchester	Cathedral and Collegiate Church of St Mary, St Denys and St George
Bradford	Cathedral Church of St Peter	Millport	Cathedral of the Isles and Collegiate Church of the Holy Spirit
Brecon	Cathedral Church of St John the Evangelist	Newcastle	Cathedral Church of St Nicholas
Bristol	Cathedral Church of the Holy and Undivided Trinity	Newport	Cathedral Church of St Woolos
Canterbury	Cathedral and Metropolitical Church of Christ	Norwich	Cathedral Church of the Holy and Undivided
Carlisle	Cathedral Church of the Holy and Undivided Trinity	Oban	St John the Divine Cathedral
Chelmsford	Cathedral Church of St Mary the Virgin, St Peter and St Cedd	Oxford	Cathedral Church of Christ
Chester	Cathedral Church of Christ and the blessed Virgin Mary	Perth	St Ninnian Cathedral
Chichester	Cathedral Church of the Holy Trinity	Peterborough	Cathedral Church of St Peter, St Paul and St A
Clogher	Cathedral Church of St Macartan	Portsmouth	Cathedral Church of St Thomas of Canterbur
Coventry	Cathedral Church of St Michael	Ripon	Cathedral Church of St Peter and St Wilfrid
Derby	Cathedral Church of All Saints	Rochester	Cathedral Church of Christ and the Blessed V
Derry	Cathedral Church of St Columb	St Albans	Cathedral and Abbey Church of St Alban
Down	Cathedral Church of the Holy and Undivided Trinity	St Asaph	Cathedral Church of St Kentigern and St Asap
Dromore	Cathedral Church of Christ the Redeemer	St Davids	Cathedral Church of St Andrew and St David
Dundee	St Paul's Cathedral	St Edmundsbury and Ipswich	Cathedral Church of St James
Durham	Cathedral Church of Christ and the Blessed Mary the Virgin	Salisbury	Cathedral Church of the Blessed Virgin Mary
Edinburgh	Cathedral Church of St Mary	Sheffield	Cathedral Church of St Peter and St Paul
Ely	Cathedral Church of the Holy and Undivided Trinity	Sodor and Man	Cathedral Church of St German
Enniskillen	Cathedral Church of St Macartin	Southwark	Cathedral and Collegiate Church of St Saviour and St Mary Overie
Exeter	Cathedral Church of St Peter	Southwell	Cathedral and Parish Church of the Blessed Virgin Mary
Glasgow	St Mary's Cathedral	Truro	Cathedral Church of St Mary
Gloucester	Cathedral Church of St Peter and the Holy and Indivisible Trinity	Wakefield	Cathedral Church of All Saints
Guildford	Cathedral Church of the Holy Spirit	Winchester	Cathedral Church of the Holy Trinity and St Peter
Hereford	Cathedral Church of the Blessed Virgin Mary and St Ethelbert	Worcester	Cathedral Church of Christ and the Blessed Virgin Mary
Inverness	St Andrews Cathedral	York	Cathedral Church of St Peter
Leicester	Cathedral Church of St Martin		

The Church of England - The Scottish Episcopal Church - The Church of Ireland - The Church in Wales

First published in Great Britain in 2000
by Jaydem Books
Winkinswood Farm
West Sussex
RH14 0PQ

A catalogue record for this book is available from the British Library.

ISBN 1903368006

Designed by Geoffrey A.J.Butcher FCSD
Printed by Eurolitho, Milan

Cover illustration: Ely Cathedral by Charles Bone P.P.R.I., A.R.C.A

Charles Bone's Watercolours of

CATHEDRALS

All the Anglican Cathedrals in the United Kingdom

with a foreword by The Archbishop of Canterbury

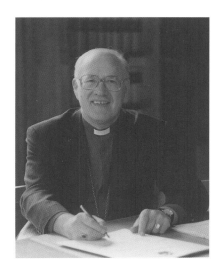

One of the jewels in the crown of Anglicanism in these islands is our Cathedrals. Not only are many of them architectural masterpieces, dating back to the earliest centuries of the Christian Faith in this country, but, more importantly, they are places where prayer has been offered up by generation after generation, and vibrant active congregations still worship today.

Charles Bone is to be congratulated on capturing much of that sense of life and vitality in this wonderful series of paintings and I am sure that this is a book that will be treasured in many homes for years to come.

✝ George Cantuar

INTRODUCTION

The cathedrals of England are amongst our finest buildings and a symbol of faith through the centuries. They are at the very roots of our civilisation. The cathedrals are the centre of the diocese and the word (cathedra) means the throne of a bishop. The medieval cathedral had the following objectives - daily offering of prayer and praise to God, the pursuit of sacred learning and continuing standards of sacred music.

Although the intellectuals of the medieval period had freedom of travel, the majority of people could not read and were moreover restricted in their movements. But they could get to a church or cathedral, and it was in these buildings where the first books, paintings and music were seen and heard by most. To the local congregation and the pilgrim, much younger than those of today, the churches and cathedrals became the equivalent of our National Gallery, Albert Hall and university.

Craftsmen moved from one centre to another producing remarkably high standards of work. Stone masons, creators, sculptors, stained glass designers and silversmiths, the artist who painted the mural and the illuminated manuscript were all travelling. The craftsmen in clay too, would construct their kilns near the site and once enough tiles and vessels had been made, would move on to the next town. It was easier to move the potter than the wares.

In the Middle Ages, cathedrals were often surrounded by battlements. Lincoln Cathedral Close, for example, was surrounded by a 12ft wall. From the Cathedral Rolls we gather that to quarry stone was both costly and difficult to transport and so local stone was used where possible. The pale magnesium limestone brought from Tadcaster to York or the limestone for Durham meant that local materials did help blend the buildings themselves into the landscape in a sympathetic way.

Theodore of Tarsus came to Canterbury with a great collection of Greek and Latin books and ever since libraries became an essential part of learning and many great libraries and estates were granted to the cathedrals. William de St Carileph, for example, the first Bishop of Durham left his books to the diocese. Ecclesiastics were often great collectors and although many books were distributed to colleges and later to museums after the dissolution, there remains a rich heritage, like the Morley Library at Winchester, containing the bible written in Latin and illuminated in the 12th century.

As places of education, the cathedrals developed colleges, such as Christ Church Oxford and Winchester.

The year 2000 is a symbolic date. Historians are not agreed on the precise date of the birth of Christ as the Romans redesigned the calendar. What is not in dispute, however, is the need for and the value of religion through the centuries and there is no better illustration of this than our enduring cathedrals. They have all suffered, at different times, at the hands of reformers or the military but they are still with us.

The production of drawings for this book proved difficult at times due to weather and on arrival parts of the cathedral would be covered in scaffolding, a constant reminder of how much continuing work is needed to safeguard the fabric of these buildings. The historic notes in the book are just to whet the readers' appetite as many specialist books exist on the art and architecture of these marvellous buildings.

I would like to thank the Deans and Chapters of these cathedrals for their kindness in helping me prepare this book, and for their permission to reproduce the cathedral symbols.

ST ANDREWS CATHEDRAL
ABERDEEN

t Andrews Cathedral is of the Diocese of Aberdeen and Orkney, one of the seven dioceses of the Scottish Episcopal Church. Early records are lost but a congregation existed in 1716 when Andrew Jaffrey became minister. On the 14th November Samuel Seabury of Connecticut was consecrated Bishop for America and was the first bishop outside the British Isles to be consecrated of what in now referred to as the Anglican Communion.

Seabury's consecration by John Skinner, Bishop Kilgour of Aberdeen and Bishop Petrie of Moray forced legislation from parliament and the Church of England, making possible the establishment of bishops for the colonies. This was an important development.

Archibald Simpson, born in Aberdeen and famous for his planning of the new district of Edinburgh, was the architect of St Andrew's Church, which opened in 1817 to become the Cathedral Church of the Diocese in 1914. To mark the 150th anniversary of Seabury's consecration plans were proposed in the 1920s to build a new cathedral. The Bishop and Provost crossed the Atlantic to raise funds but the Wall Street crash put an end to this plan and the extension of the existing building was pursued instead.

Decorated in 1935, an impressive ceiling displays the arms of the 48 States of America, and among flags displayed with an American connection there is a regimental colour presented by General Eisenhower. The Arms of Connecticut are above the Seabury Stall on the north side of the chancel and on the ceiling are the arms of George VI and Queen Elizabeth the Queen Mother.

The guilded baldachino, designed by Sir Ninian Comper, dominates the sanctuary and to the north of the altar is the foundation stone of the Seabury monument which was laid by Joseph Kennedy in 1938, accompanied by his 21 year old son John, later to become President.

At the west end of the south aisle stands the sculpture by the eminent Royal Academician John Flaxman of Bishop Skinner to commemorate his initiative in America. The Seabury Chalice and Paten was a gift from the American church, presented in 1884 at the Centenary celebrations. The Chalice is inscribed "Connecticut to Scotland AD1784 - AD 1884. A grateful memorial before God of the Episcopate and Eucharistic Office transmitted by Bishops Kilgour, Petrie and Skinner to Seabury and the Church in America. Think upon them Our God for good according to all that they have done for this people."

When the Church of Scotland reciprocated and presented Bishop William of Connecticut with a pastoral staff, members of the Episcopal Synod responded enthusiastically in St Andrews's Church.

CATHEDRAL CHURCH OF ST PATRICK ARMAGH

The early church, reputed to be built by St Patrick, was a rare stone building as most churches at this time were timber-thatched. It was therefore known as Damhliag Mor or great stone church. According to the Book of Armagh it measured 140 feet in length and it was in 447AD that St Patrick ordained that it should have pre-eminence over all Irish churches, a position which has remained unchanged.

A granite slab on the exterior of the west wall commemorates the burial of Brian Boroimhe (Boru) High King of Ireland who, in 1014, was responsible for the final defeat of the Danish power in Ireland.

After the Danish invaders' burning and an unfortunate fire caused by lightning, most of the cathedral was roofless for 130 years. Re-roofed by Archbishop Celsus, it was once again destroyed by fire, and on this ancient site the church has been re-built at least 17 times. Primate O'Scanlan began serious re-building in 1261, and there is still some evidence in the foundations today.

The North Transept is used as a Chapter House and contains some early iron age sculpture and medieval carved stones and the north window contains armorial bearings of benefactors of the 1834 restoration. The remains of an 11th century Celtic cross stands in the west end of the aisle, evidence of early Christian worship.

The 18th century physician Sir Thomas Molyneux of Castle Dillon is the subject of a very fine statue by Louis Francois Roubiliac, an important sculptor who has works in the Victoria and Albert Museum.

In the North Aisle is the monument to Dr Peter Drelincourt Dean of Armagh carved by the Flemish sculptor John Michael Rysbrack.

One of the two carved oak chairs, called the Bramhall Chair named after Archbishop John Bramhall, is used for the consecration of Bishops and the ordaining of priests and deacons. The carving of the crown on the top symbolises the restoration of the sovereign and is dated 1661. Of interest in the south aisle is the marble bust of Archbishop Robertson 1765-1794 by Joseph Nollekens 1737-1823, a leading English sculptor.

During the Reformation many relics were publicly burnt in the High Street in Dublin. Two remaining are the bell of St Patrick and the Book of Armagh now in the Library of Trinity College. The original crozier of St Patrick, known as Bachal Isa, was destroyed. Lewis Nockalls Cottingham, a notable architect of his day, was employed to restore the cathedral in 1834. He removed the old spire and rebuilt piers and arches. Some walls were as much as 21 inches out of line and had to be straightened using heated irons. The clerestory windows were uncovered after years of concealment, giving a completely new look.

Thackeray visited Armagh after the restoration and noted that it was a neat, small, fresh and handsome church, carved in the style of the 13th century and covered with gilding but felt that time, perhaps as much as 100 years, would mellow the effect.

CATHEDRAL CHURCH OF ST DEINIOL BANGOR

t Deiniol built his first church on this site in 525AD and in 546AD his church became a cathedral and he became Bishop. The number of times the church was rebuilt over the next 400 years is unknown but what is known is that the Vikings destroyed the church in 1073. Gruffudd ap Cynan regained his Kingdom of Gwynedd and restored order, then rebuilding began. The earliest surviving evidence of this period is a window built at the time of Bishop David in 1139. It is supposed that this early building was partially destroyed by the soldiers of King John who burnt Bangor in 1210.

At the end of the 13th century Bishop Anian enlarged the south transept and built a presbytery. The north transept was extended early in the 14th century and more destruction occurred in 1202 at the time of Owain Glyndwr. The western tower and a nave arcade of six bays were built under the direction of Bishop Skevington Abbot of Beaulieu in 1509.

In the cathedral library of over 4000 books, now in the hands of University College, the most important volume is Bishop Anian's Pontifical, dating from the 14th century and written on vellum with illuminations in blue and green enriched with gold leaf. The Pontifical contains the services performed by bishops, which includes ordination, confirmation and the consecration of churches.

The statue of Christ the King is positioned on the north wall of the presbytery and is one of seven statues of Flemish origin found and restored in 1961, but unbelievably discarded in the 17th century.

The six cathedrals of the Church of Wales are featured in a fine mural by Brian Thomas. Several unusual 14th century incised tiles were found by Gilbert Scott who had copies made, three can be seen set into the chancel floor. One of them shows an eagle with two heads holding a fish, the fish being an early symbol of Christianity and believed to be the emblem of the Coel Hen tribe of early Christians with which Deiniol was associated.

The early 19th century saw a great increase in Bangor's population as well as growth in English visitors, making it essential to extend the seating capacity of the cathedral. Sir George Gilbert Scott was consulted and reconstruction of the choir, transepts and chapter house was put in hand, the design being based on fragments of masonry found from the 14th century. He had also planned the building of a tower and spire but this was abandoned through lack of funds.

CATHEDRAL CHURCH OF ST ANDREW IN WELLS
BATH AND WELLS

The small city of Wells sits in the shadow of the Mendip Hills, deriving its name from the three springs near the Bishop's Palace. Evidence of Roman and Saxon burial places were discovered in Wells. The Diocese of Wells was founded in 909 and the church, founded by Aldhelm, Bishop of Sherborne, became the First Cathedral Church of St Andrew. This building fell into decay and a new cathedral was created under the direction of Bishop Robert of Lewes by extending and repairing the old building. The Saxon font is the oldest feature in the present cathedral.

The Bishop of Bath, Reginald de Bohun, 1174-1191 started the present building north of the old cathedral, but the new church did not have cathedral status at this time as the Cathedra or Bishop's Throne was still at the Abbey in Bath. A very ambitious concept for Wells, the building work began in 1179 and took 80 years to complete.

Work continued with further extensions to the Quire in 1320, where the misericords of the wooden stalls are mid-14th century and full of delightful woodcarvings. The great golden window is a fine example of medieval glass dating from the mid-14th century. Effigies of Saxon bishops were created in 1200, when the relics were moved from the old cathedral site.

After the dedication in 1244/1245 the Pope decreed that the Bishop should be named Bath and Wells, Wells becoming a cathedral once again. When the Abbey in Bath was dissolved in 1539 Wells was able to survive as the cathedral.

In the Lady Chapel, a feature in medieval cathedrals, the octagonal design completed in 1326 contained the complicated ribbed roof vault. Some original designs of the medieval glass survive here, others are compiled from fragments collected after the ravages of the Civil War.

In 1333 Dean John Godelee added further extensions to the central tower, but the foundations began to move because of the additional weight and Master Mason William Joy was called in to solve the problem, adding great scissor arches, which are a great feature of Wells. This proved to be a permanent solution.

The West Front was built to house Wells' remarkable sculptures, a most comprehensive insight into medieval life. Saints, bishops, nobles, kings and legendary characters of the scriptures are illustrated with such artistry. In recent years Professor Baker did much to conserve the statues and within the cathedral is a woodcarving of the crucifix by Jim Clack.

The astronomical clock installed in the late 14th century is in working order. Jack Blandiver kicks the bell every fifteen minutes and the jousting begins on horseback on the hour by a quartet of mounted figures.

CATHEDRAL CHURCH OF ST ANNE
BELFAST

In 1613 when Belfast was a small village it was constituted a corporation by the Royal Charter of King James 1. Half a century later, the population was only 589 but by 1780 this had increased to 13,000 and, at about this time, the first parish church of St Ann was built, replacing the older corporation church in the High Street. In 1888 the rank of City was conferred on Belfast by Queen Victoria and a proposal to build a cathedral was announced and the foundation stone was laid in 1899, the nave being consecrated on 2 June 1904, built around the old building.

The tympanum above the interior of the Great West Door is a mosaic of five angels on a background of gold tessera - a memorial to those choristers who died in the 1914-1918 War. The mosaic roof of the Bapistry contains 150,000 pieces of glass, a magnificent achievement in the Romanesque style. In the Chapel of the Holy Spirit, the decoration illustrates St Patrick passing the Mountains of Mourne on his way to Saul, holding in his hand a cross to invoke divine aid for his mission.

The capitals of the pillars are carved with subjects representing different aspects of life, while on the north side of the nave there are illustrations of great scientists, Roger Bacon, Archimedes, Isaac Newton and Lord Kelvin. Another carving depicts one of the industries of Belfast, illustrating all parts of the linen trade, pulling flax, a woman spinning, another weaving a loom and the Irish market place where the linen was sold. Perhaps the most important is the carving on the capital concerned with ship building, a major industry in the area. The design describes the history of shipbuilding from Noah's Ark to a modern oil-burning ship.

The North Transept of the cathedral was finally completed in 1881, 77 years after its first opening. This part of the building was consecrated in the presence of HRH Princess Alexandra together with a very large and grateful congregation.

CATHEDRAL CHURCH OF ST PHILIP BIRMINGHAM

The Cathedral Church of St Philip stands at the heart of the city surrounded by shopping precincts and very much part of Birmingham's daily life. It is now the oldest complete building in Birmingham.

During the reign of Queen Anne in 1708, a new parish was created named Hightown, a site for the new parish church was chosen and the architect, Thomas Archer, appointed. (His estate was at Uberslade Hall, about 12 miles from the city.) Very much influenced by Italian architecture following his experience on the Grand Tour, Archer returned to design a church tower, described by Nicholas Pevsner as a rare example of English Baroque. It was in fact modelled on the central dome of Santa Maria della Salute in Venice, a church built in the mid-17th century by Longhena. The new parish church was consecrated in 1715, costing £5,000 6s 4d.

Today, the original galleries remain but the chandeliers date from 1905 when St Philip's became a Cathedral. During the 19th century, Birmingham became the world centre for metal industries, congregations increased and the Chancel was added to the east end in 1884, designed by J A Chatwin. At the same time, the organ was installed and choir stalls constructed. Under theologian Bishop Charles Gore, a separate See was created to give Birmingham new status.

Sir Edward Burne-Jones, the great pre-Raphelite was baptised in St Philips and through the generosity of Miss Emma Chadwick Villiers Wilkes, money was available to finance the magnificent east windows by Burne-Jones. These windows allowed colour and light to flood into the building, an early application of the arts and crafts movement associated with Sir Edward's Oxford friend, William Morris. The four windows are divided, three at the east end - Nativity, Ascension and Crucifixion - and alone at the west end, the Last Judgement.

Another significant historical event - the American Revolution of 1776 - is remembered by a tablet on one of the Nave's north piers, depicting Peter Oliver, Lord Chief Justice in Massachusetts, who decided his loyalties were with the Crown. He died in exile in Birmingham.

During World War II the Cathedral was bombed and set on fire, but fortunately the Burne-Jones windows had been removed and stored in a Welsh mine shaft. Despite being roofless the Cathedral held prayers throughout the war. J H Richards, Provost of the Cathedral from 1937-48, was subsequently responsible for the restoration of the building when the war ended. It was the Provost's own house which was used by returning World War II servicemen for rest and companionship.

For 300 years the Cathedral has been at the centre of Birmingham's civic tradition. It provides the regular meeting place for a number of organisations - the Pre-Raphelite Society, the Birmingham International Council and the Birmingham and Pakistan Friendship Society. The large numbers of tourists and pilgrims visiting the city are able to watch a regular cycle of Mystery Plays.

The blind and partially sighted can explore the Cathedral's wide range of architectural features using the lime wood model and plan which has been hand-crafted to a precise scale. This is part of the "Cathedral Through Touch and Hearing" project launched by the University of Birmingham.

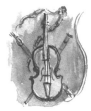

CATHEDRAL CHURCH OF ST MARY THE VIRGIN BLACKBURN

 t Mary the Virgin is the only Anglican cathedral in Lancashire. Although Christian worship has occurred on this site since 596AD the diocese was not created until 1926 when the vision of architect W A Forsyth turned the parish church into a cathedral, complete with spacious transepts.

The original Georgian building, extended to accommodate the services of a cathedral, contained a nave which retains its unique and beautiful Georgian ceiling. Above the high altar is a suspended corona weighing four tons and made in steel, representing a crown of glory and a crown of thorns, a memorial to Canon John Sinker, the first Provost here.

Three factors led to the selection of Blackburn as the central church of the diocese:- the existing church was large and in the centre of the town, there was plenty of surrounding land to extend the building and the east end allowed for an undercroft. Forsyth was responsible for work on the cathedral between the two World Wars but after the last war the plans had to be revised for economic reasons and Lawrence King was appointed the architect in 1961. He had an unenviable task but his imaginative response was to prove successful.

The floor of the nave is constructed of Derbyshire limestone, giving a natural finish. Delicate columns are constructed of stone quarried at nearby Longridge. High on the west wall of the nave is a sculpture of Christ the Worker, wearing a scapular, a monastic cloak worn during manual labour and in the background is a symbolic stylised loom, the work of John Haywood. Lancashire's wealth was founded on spinning and weaving.

The east window, designed by John Haywood brings light and colour into the building. Set in a window in the south transept are small fragments of Medieval glass, remnants of the Tudor church after Cromwellian forces had smashed the contents of the building on their return to the Yorkshire borders. These are set into clear glass panels and are of outstanding quality.

The Medieval Pax Madonna, just 2½" high was discovered in 1820 when a tombstone was removed. This has become the emblem of the Friends of the Cathedral.

The altar frontal is quite unique with four embroidered panels based on an ornithological theme - the phoenix, the dove, the pelican and the peacock. The design was masterminded by Mrs Dorothy Anderson and the work created by the Diocesan Fellowship of church needleworkers.

The north transept displays a sculpture of the Virgin and Child by Josephina Vasconcellos. The original bishop's throne was constructed by Advent Hunston and bears the arms of the cathedral diocese and that of Manchester, Chester and Lichfield.

The cathedral has several historic chalices, which are still in constant use. One dates from Elizabethan times and two are from the reign of Charles I.

Eight new stained glass panels, designed by Linda Walton, are positioned in the cathedral lantern, the theme is fire and water and this beacon can be seen throughout the city.

CATHEDRAL CHURCH OF ST PETER BRADFORD

In 1919 the Bradford Diocese was born out of the Diocese of Ripon and Bradford Parish Church became a cathedral. However, the remains of a Saxon preaching cross suggests that Christians have worshipped here since 627AD, the date of Paulinus' mission to Northumbria.

Paulinus preached at Dewsbury in 627AD and from there Bradford was evangelised. The Parish of Bradford is recorded in the register of York in 1281 and Alice de Lacy gave a grant to the parish. Following the Norman timber framed church the stone church still existed here and was reputed to be destroyed by raiders from Scotland.

The 14th century saw the complete rebuilding. In line with common practice at the time, materials were re-used in the construction. The nave arcades were completed by 1458, the perpendicular style tower was added and completed in 1508. During the sieges of Bradford the church was involved with the Civil War. Parliamentarians of Bradford successfully defeated Royalist attempts to overthrow them and during a fierce battle protected the church tower from canon fire by hanging wool sacks over the building. The wool sacks can be seen illustrated as part of the shield of the Diocese.

A tablet on the north aisle wall was given on the 700th anniversary of the granting of a market charter by Henry III. The magnificent medieval font cover was restored in York and hangs on a pulley from the roof of the south west corner of the nave. Part of the sanction preaching cross was built into the cathedral wall together with a piscina found during the rebuilding in 1963 and a stone engraved with sheep shears is a reminder of the wool trade that brought prosperity to Bradford in the early days.

Close to the church a canal link was formed to the main Leeds Liverpool Canal, bringing trade and prosperity to Bradford. A memorial on the east side of the north door shows Joseph Priestley supervising the work with the picks and shovels digging the cut.

The stained glass windows in the Lady Chapel were made by Morris Marshall Faulkner and Company. William Morris designed some of the figures and the angels in the tracery lights. Other sections are by Rossetti, Ford, Madox Brown, Webb and Peter Marshall, and though most of this glass has been replaced in the new setting, a few of Morris's angels are now in the Whitworth Art Gallery in Manchester.

A roundel on the east wall of the north transept shows the response of an appeal to assist those who suffered in the Bradford City Football Ground fire disaster on May 11 1985. 56 people died and 300 were injured. The cathedral became the focal point in the city when a service was taken by the Bishop on the following day.

CATHEDRAL CHURCH OF ST JOHN THE EVANGELIST BRECON

In an area of outstanding natural beauty, overlooking the market town of Brecon and the Honddu River, the present building has stood over 900 years. The church was originally part of the Benedictine Priory and became the Cathedral Church of the Diocese of Swansea and Brecon in 1923. The Diocese evolved out of the ancient See of St David's, when the Church of Wales divided from the Church of England to become a separate province of Anglican Communion.

After defeating the Welsh in 1093, the Norman Bernard de Neufmarche built a castle in Brecon and through his influence a priory and church, together with monastic quarters, were established north-east of the castle on the site of the present church. Some early stone work and the font are the only remains of this structure.

In 1537, at the time of the Dissolution when many of the Brecon treasurers were destroyed and the richly painted decorations in the church lime-washed over, John Price became the Inspector of Monasteries in Wales for the Crown and converted the Prior's house into his own residence.

The approach to the cathedral is dominated by the massive defensive wall, a necessary part of medieval construction. At the top of the hill, the tithe barn with its grotesque gargoyles and mullioned windows, is now a very fine Heritage Centre, visited by many walking the National Park. The exhibits include the cresset stone, a medieval form of lighting, as well as artefacts and a recorded history of cathedral life.

In the north aisle of the cathedral near the 16th century carved cabinet, is the sole remaining guild chapel of the Corbizors (shoe makers), probably dedicated to the patron saints of S S Crispin and Crispinian, and now called St Keynes Chapel. A dormer window here has the figures of Brychan, Cynog and Alud, the early pioneers of Christianity in these parts.

The oldest part of the present building is the early English chancel dating from 1201, where the east window commemorates officers and men of the South Wales Borderers killed in the Zulu War. On the south side is a very rare triple piscina, used for the cleaning of altar vessels. The stone reredos, carved by W D Caroe, is based on designs of the 16th century and makes an imposing feature.

Elsewhere in the cathedral are wall memorials by John Flaxman RA, better known for his designs on the Wedgwood Jasperware. Amongst the gravestones and tombs in the churchyard is a reference to a British soldier, one of the first to be awarded the Victoria Cross, and a French officer who died in Brecon during the Napoleonic wars.

CATHEDRAL CHURCH OF THE HOLY AND UNDIVIDED TRINITY - BRISTOL

Robert Fitzhardinge, ancestor of the Earls of Berkeley, together with six canons founded the Augustinian abbey in 1140 and about 1165 the abbey church was consecrated. Some original buildings including the Chapter House were constructed in Norman times and survive to this day. The eastern end of the church was rebuilt between 1298 and 1330 and the magnificent central tower was completed in 1500.

The central tower contains the original bell frame and three bells. The other bells were melted down by order of Edward VI, presumably for the bronze, much valued for the production of arms. The Elder Lady Chapel, so called because of its existence prior to the new structure built in 1298, has delightful carvings of animals, birds, St Michael and the Dragon and an amusing monkey playing the pipes. Nearby is the tomb of the ninth Lord Berkeley and his mother. He was wounded, captured by the French at Poitiers, and for four years was held for ransom, finally returning to Bristol to die in 1368.

The eastern Lady Chapel was restored in 1935 by Professor Tristram, my first professor at the Royal College of Art. Also here we see a window showing the arms of Lord Berkeley and his relatives who fought at the Battle of Crécy.

Effigies of 15th century abbots surround the walls, among them the builder of the central tower, Abbot Newbery and Abbot Newland, responsible for the Refectory and Gate House. A 14th century glass illustrates the martyrdom of St Edmund killed by the Danes.

The dissolution of the monasteries by Henry VIII curtailed any future expansion and in 1542 the new diocese of Bristol was formed and the church became a cathedral. In 1712, two candlesticks were given to the cathedral, now positioned on the altar, as a thanksgiving for the safe return of two ships, the Duke and the Duchess, after circumnavigating the world to bring back Alexander Selkirk from the Juan Fernandez Islands. He was to become the inspiration for Robinson Crusoe.

Reconstruction of the nave was under way in the Middle Ages but never completed. However, in 1868 G E Street began work on the original foundations of 1500, creating what is referred to in Germany as a Hall Church with a roof of the same height, the only example in England.

Elsewhere, there is a notable monument to the poet Robert Southey, and in the South Transept a replacement window by Keith New, the original suffering damage in the Second World War.

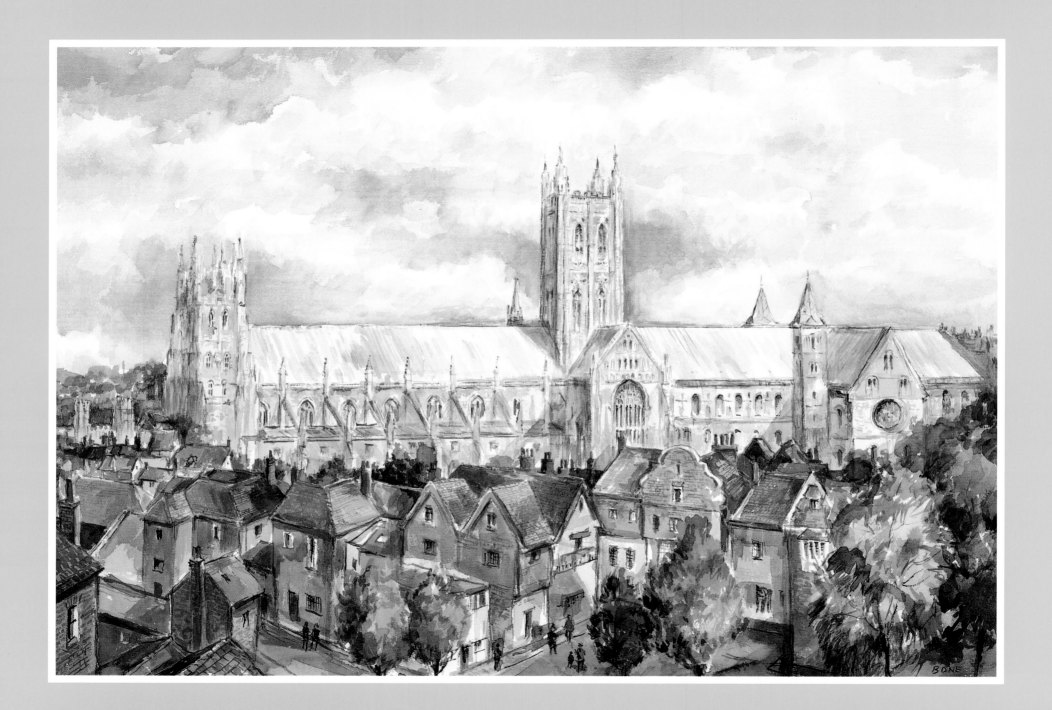
BONE

CATHEDRAL AND METROPOLITICAL CHURCH OF CHRIST CANTERBURY

After 14 centuries of damage or near destruction by fire, invading armies or the zeal of reformers, the Cathedral Church of Christ faced its stiffest test in the first week of June 1942, when high-explosive bombs dropped on its Precincts. The building emerged, again, almost untouched.

It was the murder of Thomas Becket in 1170 which left a far more lasting impression on Canterbury, and which gave it its pre-eminence in the Christian world.

Previous Archbishops, Augustine, Lanfranc and Anselm, had played their part, but when Becket was slain by the four knights William de Tracy, Reginald Fitzurse, Richard le Breton and Hugh de Morville all Christendom was horrified, the deed enduringly reflected in letters, in politics and in art.

For 350 years, Canterbury would be visited by pilgrims from all over the world, the largest numbers, like Chaucer's 29 tellers of Tales, journeying from London. With the cathedral full, masses had to be suspended, but the city was profiting with so many pilgrims requiring lodging.

The hollows in the steps leading to Trinity Chapel were worn down by the tread of countless pilgrims visiting the gold and gem laden St Thomas' Shrine from 1220 until its destruction in 1538. The mosaic floor is indented by the toes of the pilgrims as they knelt.

One of the first visitors was Louis VII in 1179, symbolising French approval of Becket's shrine, adding to the reputation of England's internationally celebrated saint.

Six centuries before, Augustine accompanied by his 40 Benedictine monks from Rome, had landed in Kent to become the first Archbishop of the Cathedral of Canterbury.

Fire was to ravage the building twice. In 1067, the first cathedral was destroyed with much of the monastery, but rebuilt when William the Conqueror appointed the 70 year old Abbot of Caen, Lanfranc, as Archbishop. Then, under the aegis of the next Archbishop Anselm a glorious new Norman Quire was constructed, only to be destroyed by fire only four years after Becket's murder.

Also entombed in the Trinity Chapel is that most spectacular of Medieval figures, Edward the Black Prince, and opposite Edward lies Henry IV, who was to overthrow the Black Prince's son, Richard II, and reign in his place.

Centuries later, in 1946, another monarch, King George VI, would attend a thanksgiving service to celebrate the wartime preservation of the cathedral. It had survived unscathed once more.

BONE

CATHEDRAL CHURCH OF THE HOLY AND UNDIVIDED TRINITY CARLISLE

Stones from the Roman City or Hadrian's Wall are now built into the walls of this ancient structure, and fragments of an 8th century cross have been excavated in the vicinity amongst other evidence of Christian burials.

In 686 AD St Cuthbert, Bishop of Lindisfarne, had jurisdiction in Carlisle, which later came under Scottish control until 1092. Carlisle diocese was founded in 1133. The majority of cathedrals in medieval times were administered by Benedictine monks, but Carlisle was unique in England being served by Augustinian canons.

The present church was founded by Henry I who endowed it in 1122 as a priory of Augustinian canons. In 1133 the King established the Diocese of Carlisle making this church its cathedral. The Norman quire was rebuilt on a grander scale in the 13th century and in 1292 a fire destroyed much of the building. As a result a great deal of rebuilding was necessary in the 14th century. Further devastation occurred in 1650 when parliamentary troops demolished the five bays of the nave and used the stone to rebuild the city's fortifications.

In Bishop Strickland's time (1400-1419) a new tower was constructed as the Norman one had collapsed. It was during his episcopate that the elaborate carving on the 15th century stalls was put in place. These were originally painted and gilded carved figures in the niches.

In the North Transept, St Wilfred's Chapel displays the Brougham Triptych carved in Antwerp about 1515, illustrating vividly the Passion of Christ. Acquired by Lord Brougham the then Lord Chancellor in the 1830s, it is on loan from Brougham Parish and is one of only a few such works in Britain. The great East Window is reported to be the finest example of tracery in the country.

A sculpture of the Virgin and Child titled "I am the life" by Josephina de Vasconcellos is situated in the North Nave Aisle.

Painted panels of saints on the back of the choir stalls, dating from the late 15th century, serve as a reminder that all the woodwork and stonework was painted in the medieval period.

In 1297 Edward I received the allegiance of Robert the Bruce, sworn upon the sword that supposedly killed Thomas Becket in Canterbury. During excavations below the nave to accommodate the Treasury, a jet crucifix was discovered amongst the archaeological remains. The Verge, reputed to have been used by Bishop Oglethorpe at the Coronation of Elizabeth I, is on display in the Treasury, together with a fine medieval cope dating from 1440. Also on display in the chapel of St Catherine is the charming 15th century screen associated with Prior Gondebour.

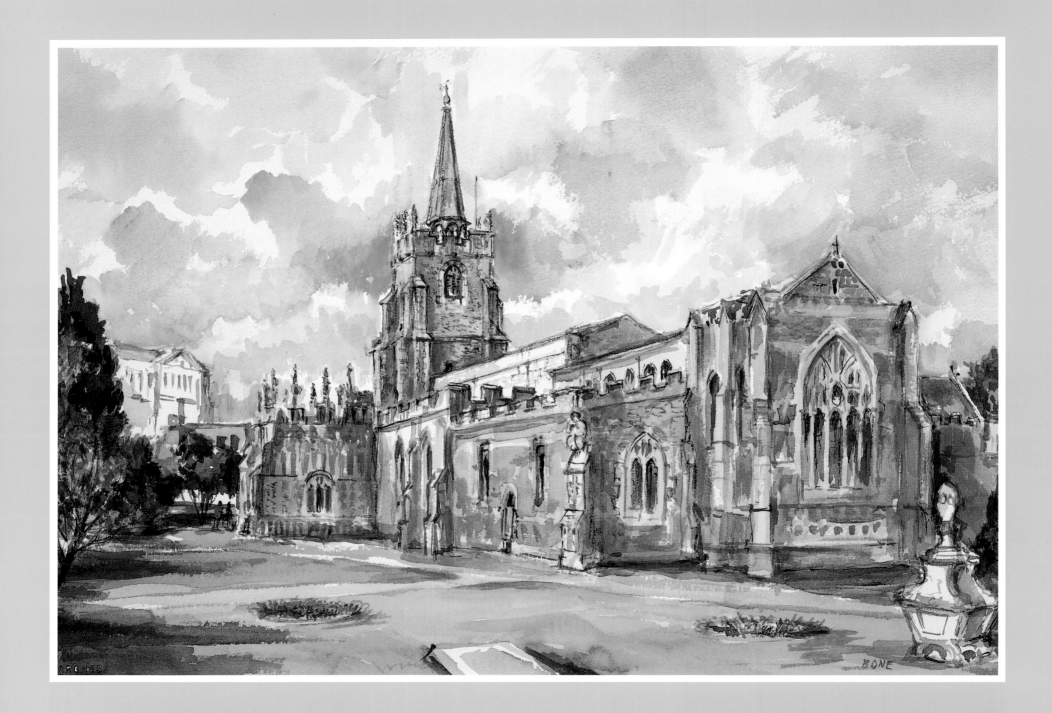

CATHEDRAL CHURCH OF ST MARY THE VIRGIN, ST PETER AND ST CEDD - CHELMSFORD

t Cedd, a bishop according to Bede, built large churches in this area, including St Peter's on the Wall at Bradwell on Sea. Travel in this marshy area at the time proved very difficult but in 1087 the river was bridged and since it was on the route from London to Colchester the town developed.

The Norman Bishop William held the rural manor on the east of the River Chelmer. In the 12th century the first church was built, dedicated to St Mary, serving Chelmsford and Moulsham, south of the river. With the expanding town the church was considered too small and in the 16th century complete rebuilding began, which continued with alterations and developments for the next 500 years.

The church suffered the effects of the Civil War and in 1641 the sum of £5 was paid to remove the representations of the Virgin Mary and Christ from the Great East Window. Bells were rung to celebrate the failure of Guido Fawkes in 1605, but that evening the church was vandalised and the remaining glass in the east window destroyed. The wooden carved angel was removed and burnt in the street and at one time the Rector was thrown into a grave whilst conducting a burial service. He finally fled to Oxford.

The tower is 29 metres high and the spire was rebuilt in 1744. The weather vane is also from this date. The 16 stone carvings and the foot of the battlements are by Huxley Jones.

Population expansion in London in the 19th century created the need to form a separate diocese. This was created by an Act of Parliament and by the vote of various parishes in the locality Chelmsford was adopted as the new cathedral. John Watts Ditchfield was the first bishop in 1914 and the diocese is now the second largest in population. Many additions have been made to the building to accommodate the space required for cathedral services and in 1990 a new Chapter House was added to provide facilities for diocesan cathedral and community use.

In the cathedral is a monument to Thomas Mildmay and his family, dating from 1566. Thomas's father came to Chelmsford in 1506 and acquired a market stall, eventually becoming one of the wealthiest men in Chelmsford. His son was appointed an auditor, controlling revenue from the devolved monastic properties, subsequently acquiring the Manor of Chelmsford.

20th century sculptors and artists have works in the cathedral. A stone sculpture by John Skelton FRBS stands in front of the bishop's chair. The cathedral banner with strong Byzantine influence took Beryl Dean 800 hours to complete and in St Peter's Chapel is a bronze called "The bond child" by Georg Ehrlich, who was displaced from his native Austria by the Nazi invasion.

CATHEDRAL CHURCH OF CHRIST AND THE BLESSED VIRGIN MARY - CHESTER

Chester began as a Roman fortress about 70AD but by 907AD this important centre was derelict. It was restored in the reign of Ethelred of Mercea as a fortress against the Norsemen occupying nearby areas of the country. A church existed on the site of the present cathedral and was enlarged to house the relics of St Werburgh, daughter of King Wulfere, an abbess with a reputation for reforming holy life and to whom several miracles are attributed, and recorded on her tomb. Chester's relics meant that it soon became a centre for spiritual pilgrimage.

Hugh Lupus, Lord of the Welsh Marches, founded the Cathedral Church of Christ and the Blessed Virgin Mary in 1095 for the Benedictines, dedicated to St Werburgh and part of the diocese of Lichfield. He received help from a friend Anselm Abbott of Bec in Normandy, together with monks who accompanied him to Chester. Important work was carried out by the Benedictine monks in areas of education and caring for the elderly and orphans.

Chester received cathedral status by Henry VIII during the reorganisation of the Church of England, a somewhat rare event at this time. Built of red sandstone which is subject to weather erosion, repairs and patching and recarving were necessary even in Medieval times.

Thomas Clark became the first Dean of the new cathedral. By the 18th century the building, in serious decline, was eventually saved by the architect Sir George Gilbert Scott during the time of Dean Anson. Ranulph Higden, a Medieval monk of Chester, is buried here. He is famous for his writing on the history of the world until 1352, titled "Polychronicon", a copy of which is in the cathedral collection. A large stained glass window depicts St Anselm who assisted in the foundation of St Werburgh's Abbey in 1092; he is holding a ship, a reminder of Anselm's double exile whilst Archbishop of Canterbury under William I and Henry I.

The first important rebuilding took place between 1200 and 1315 when the eastern section was remodelled with a new Lady Chapel. The monks continued to enlarge the building in the 14th century, reconstructing the nave and central tower, until the Black Death brought the work to a premature end.

Further modifications were carried out much later by Abbott Simon Ripley 1485-1498 and by Abbott Birkenshaw 1498-1537. The feature of the cathedral is a remarkable set of choir stalls, dating from the late 14th century, which contain a perfect set of 48 misericords, carved in designs illustrating fables and a range of mythical and religious motifs.

The original monastery water tank was discovered in the present flower garden. Water was originally supplied through lead pipes from Christleton, two miles away.

CATHEDRAL CHURCH OF THE HOLY TRINITY CHICHESTER

The cathedral is built on a flat plain against a backdrop of the Sussex Downs. The spire is visible from the tidal inlets of the sea and nearby is the great Roman palace of Fishbourne and the coastal village of Bosham with its links with King Canute.

1091 marks the time of the first Norman church under Bishop Ralph de Luffa, a few years following the transfer of the Saxon See of Selsey to Chichester. Fire damage caused the collapse of the timbered roof in 1187 and this resulted in re-planning the stone vault throughout. It is possible that the craftsmen involved were trained under William of Sens and William the Englishman from Canterbury.

The Lady Chapel was increased by two bays under Bishop Gilbert de Leophardi, between 1288 and 1305 and the first spire was raised over the tower in about 1380. The cathedral has a separate bell tower, a common feature of churches and a method of solving the problem of heavy bells and mountings. As architectural skills developed the bells were positioned in the main structure. Chichester is possibly the only surviving tower in a cathedral close, since the rest were demolished, the last being Salisbury in 1790. The stone used for the construction came from the Isle of Wight.

Built into the wall of the south aisle are two 12th century Romanesque stone carvings of Christ raising Lazarus from the dead and Jesus entering the house of Martha and Mary.

These are some of the many treasures of Chichester, both discovered in rubble in 1829 and fragments of a third panel are installed in the library.

The Arundel Screen in the early perpendicular style was discarded in the last century and was rebuilt in the campanile in 1961, 500 years after its original creation.

The tomb of Bishop Robert Sherburne in the south choir aisles commemorates the bishop who was 90 years old when he died in 1536, before the disasters of the Reformation.

The 20th century is well represented in the visual arts, with two tapestries, one by John Piper and the other by Ursula Benker Schirmer and paintings by Patrick Procktor and Graham Sutherland. The font is designed by John Skelton FRBS, a sculptor from Sussex, and the pulpit by Geoffrey Clarke. There is also some very fine contemporary silver.

The town is much improved by the pedestrian areas, the market cross being a central feature. Years ago an old man told art historian Alec Clifton-Taylor that when he was a boy looking out of the train window approaching Chichester, he saw the spire of the cathedral collapse. The authorities had been informed that this might happen but no one was injured. Rebuilding was undertaken under the direction of Scott who adhered closely to the original design, the result recognised as a success.

CATHEDRAL CHURCH OF ST MACARTAN
CLOGHER

With its churchyard path once the old bridleway to Dublin, set in the heart of the Clogher Valley, lies the square-towered Cathedral of St Macartan, prominent on its green hill in North Tyrone. The Clogh-oir (a stone round which was gold) in the porch is evidence of Christian, even pre-Christian roots.

The present cathedral was built by Bishop Stearne between 1740 and 1744, largely at his own expense and using the architect-builder services of James Martin, the builder of Baronscourt. It was then remodelled and re-roofed by Dean Bagwell in 1816 and given its present plain classical appearance. Re-roofing was again necessary in 1967.

In 1950, five years after the bi-centenary celebrations, a diocesan appeal was launched by Bishop Tyner to raise over £4,000 for vital restoration work. Two years later, the exterior repairs were complete, including repointing the whole building, organ repairs and recasting of the bells. Dedication of the bells by the Bishop and the first peal was broadcast.

The cathedral was re-opened on 31 May 1956, after more than £5,000 had been contributed by parishioners and the Friends.

Clogher's original cathedral was rebuilt, after two fires in 1395 and 1396, by Bishop Arthur MacCawell. By 1517, according to a recently discovered document in the Vatican archives,

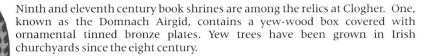

Clogher was a city of 40 houses and the cathedral 'square shaped, built of natural stone, roofed partly with wood, partly with straw'.

Clogher was wasted by wars and the See reported to be 'not worth more than 80 ducats a year'. The town was described as a 'walled city' and North Tyrone as a country of forests, lakes and swamps, 'where the dominion of England ceases and a native count reigns'.

Ninth and eleventh century book shrines are among the relics at Clogher. One, known as the Domnach Airgid, contains a yew-wood box covered with ornamental tinned bronze plates. Yew trees have been grown in Irish churchyards since the eight century.

Tradition has it, though there is no evidence, that Jonathan Swift, author of Gulliver's Travels, who was a friend of the Bishop and would often stay in Clogher, was secretly married to Stella Johnson by Bishop St George Ashe in 1716 under a lime tree.

The old churchyard holds 600 tombstones, many of them still decipherable and the cemetery contains the graves of at least six bishops as well as the mortal remains of St Macartan, the first Bishop and Abbot of Clogher. It is this link with 5th century monastic Christianity in rural Ireland which is at the root of Clogher's independent faith.

CATHEDRAL CHURCH OF ST MICHAEL COVENTRY

The original Cathedral Church of St Michael was destroyed by incendiary bombs on 14 November 1940, only the walls, tower and spire remaining relatively unharmed. The oak ceiling, pews and all of the wooden structures were destroyed. Two relics rose from the cathedral ruins - the now famous charred cross, constructed from two roof beams and the Cross of Nails, formed from three of the 14th century hand-forged nails. This has become an important symbol in international reconciliation.

The new cathedral, adjacent to the old, was designed by Sir Basil Spence and consecrated on 25 May 1962 in the presence of Her Majesty the Queen.
The Chapel of Unity was designed to encourage Christians of all denominations to worship here. Inset in the floor is the inscription "that they all may be one". The windows were designed by Margaret Traherne and were a gift from the German evangelical churches.

A large glass screen, depicting angels, saints and prophets is effectively the west wall. On each side of the nave, the subtle modelling of figures in etched glass and the five angled windows on the theme of the Revelation of God and the Destiny of Man are best viewed from the high altar. Sculptor Geoffrey Clarke designed the High Altar cross and within it lies the original Cross of Nails.

The tapestry of the majestic Figure of Christ by Graham Sutherland, is the most impressive feature and the largest in the world. It was woven in France by Pinton Frères at Felletin near Aubusson and measures 72 feet by 38 feet and weighs a ton.

The windows in the Lady Chapel were designed by Einar Forseth and presented by Sweden, symbolising the Christian Fellowship and international character of this cathedral. The Chapel of Christ the Servant, also designed by Sir Basil Spence, incorporates an oak altar table, inlaid with boxwood on a stone base; the gift and work of the Coventry Technical College, part of Sir Basil's idea of incorporating the young generation of Coventry into the new cathedral structure. The inscription reads "I am among you as one who serves".

The lectern, finished in bronze, displays a bronze eagle by Dame Elisabeth Frink, a theme which dates back to her early student days.

The great Bapistry window with 195 separate lights made by Patrick Reyntiens was designed by John Piper. The large bronze feature "St Michael and the Devil" by Sir Jacob Epstein is the last religious work he completed is placed at the entrance to the cathedral, where the porch connects the old cathedral to the new building.

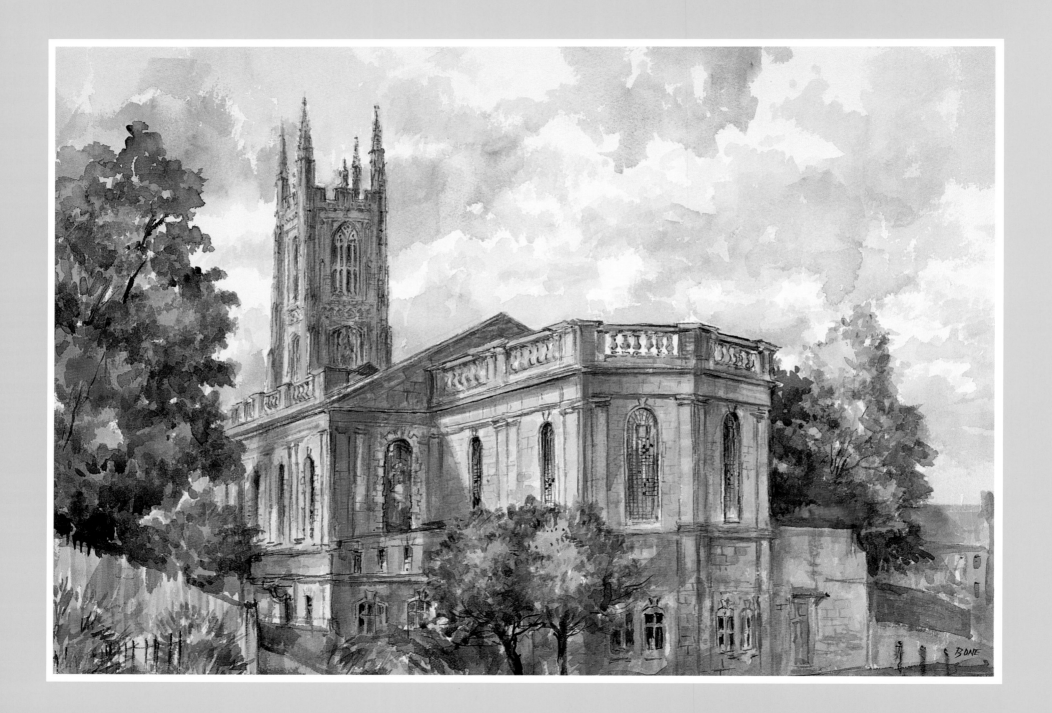

CATHEDRAL CHURCH OF ALL SAINTS
DERBY

All Saints was probably founded in 943 by King Edmund as a royal collegiate church. In the 12th century the church was given to Lincoln Cathedral by King Henry I, the Dean of Lincoln therefore becoming the Dean of All Saints.

No trace remains of the Saxon church on this site but during the 14th century a new church was built. Little is known of this but it was roughly the size of the present building. A pinnacled rectangular tower, probably unsafe, was pulled down and a replacement tower built early to mid 16th century in the perpendicular style. This is the structure you now see. In 1556 the church acquired a martyr, Joan Waste. She was blind and although she visited the church daily to have the New Testament read to her by the clerk she would not accept the doctrine of transubstantiation and under the heresy laws she was burnt.

The pre-Reformation church had at least six altars and very valuable plate. In the reign of Edward VI the college was dissolved, the priests removed and the artefacts sold. In 1556 Mary Tudor granted pensions to the unfortunate deposed canons. Bess of Hardwick, the daughter of John Hardwick of Hardwick Hall, was buried in the vault below St Katherine's. During her life she developed estates in Derbyshire, including Chatsworth, which was purchased for £600 in 1549. The house was not to her taste so £80,000 was spent on a new building of which nothing remains.

By the end of the 17th century the church was in a ruinous state and the corporation finally agreed to support a new church and invited financial contributions and started a subscription list. James Gibbs was the architect chosen. Amongst his other designs were St Martin's in the Field and St Mary-le-Strand. The architecture was in a simple, classical style married to the 16th century tower. Many of the memorials were lost in the rebuilding but some, including that of Bess of Hardwick, were reinstalled.

The church, being Royal and free, did not come under the control of the bishop of the diocese, then Lichfield and Coventry, and Episcopal friction continued into the 18th century. As a Royal Peculiar, All Saints was entitled to grant marriage licences and probate of wills. Normally a diocesan prerogative, the practice was terminated in 1857.

A new stone font was installed in 1974 and to celebrate the cathedral's diamond jubilee Rolls Royce undergraduates and apprentices designed and made a portable font in stainless steel to be moved and used when baptism is conducted in the presence of the whole congregation.

CATHEDRAL CHURCH OF ST COLUMB DERRY

t Columba was born in 521AD, a member of the reigning family of Ireland and British Dalriada. He sailed from Derry with 12 companions and founded Iona off the coast of Scotland, which became the great missionary centre, although he loved Derry above any other place.

Anglo-Norman raiders were sent by Popes Adrian IV and Alexander III to extend the boundaries of the church, resulting in the churches of St Patrick being burned and pillaged. The churches of Derry were further ravaged by John de Courcy in 1198 and the disturbances continued into the 17th century by both Anglo-Normans and the Irish.

The ancient Cathedral of St Columb built in 1164 was in a deplorable condition when visited by Government officials and Papal agents and in 1600 Sir Henry Docwra arrived to find the destruction of the building and most of the city, probably due to the explosion of a powder magazine used by the Army in 1568.

The Irish Society chose a hilltop site for the building of a new cathedral, a fine example of the mason's skill which was completed in 1633 and consecrated a year later. A unique occasion, it was a combined consecration of the building as a Parish Church and a Cathedral on the same day, providing worship for a local population of just 155 families.

Despite the damage caused by bombs and cannon balls in 1680 the cathedral has survived, helped in its restoration by a grant of £200 from William and Queen Mary. The old spire was demolished and the lead, stored for future reconstruction, was used for bullets instead.

During the siege of Derry the tower was used as a signalling station both by flags and beacons and it was also used as a gun platform. Good tidings were pealed by the oldest peal of bells in Ireland. These were recast in 1928 and remounted on an iron framework by Gillett and Johnstone of Croydon.

CATHEDRAL CHURCH OF THE HOLY AND UNDIVIDED TRINITY - DOWN

It is believed that the remains of the Patron Saint of Ireland, St Patrick, are buried here. Tradition has it that he brought Christianity to Ireland. Originally from Northern Britain, he was captured as a slave and landed on the coast of Wicklow and travelled north, where he met Díchu a local chieftain and having converted him to Christianity Díchu gave him a barn as his first church. Patrick had two principal biographers Muirchú and Tirecha'n, both writing centuries later.

The present Church of Ireland was built at Saul in 1932, a few miles from Down, to commemorate the 1500th anniversary of St Patrick's arrival. Early records exist and the earliest reference is the death of an Abbot of Down in 753 and from that point on an almost complete description exists of the abbots and bishops of the Celtic monastery occupying the hill.

The Norman knight John de Courcy set out to conquer the north as the Shrine of St Patrick was attracting great numbers of pilgrims and, as a result the area was developing. His mission accomplished, de Courcy founded several monasteries and invited the first prior, from Chester, to start work.

The main walls of the cathedral date from about 1220. On the suppression of the monasteries the cathedral was allowed to deteriorate to a ruinous state until King James I granted a Royal Charter in 1790 for a dean and chapter and that the cathedral be dedicated to the Holy Trinity.

The Marquis of Devonshire, together with Dean Annesley did much to raise funds to rebuild the cathedral by approaching the nobility of the county and the Marquis's parliamentary colleagues. King George III gave £1,000 to the restoration fund and the cathedral was finally consecrated in 1818.

With the disestablishment of the Church of Ireland in 1870 the Cathedral Chapter found itself without funds, since then the maintenance and upkeep was supported entirely by voluntary subscriptions. The relatively recent renovations in 1986/87, costing £750,000, involved removing plaster from the walls and vaulting in order to deal with the rot beneath. A new interior was then developed, based on the original work. This project is a great credit to the Diocese.

A special feature of the cathedral is the magnificent organ whose pipes almost reach the vaulted roof and is acknowledged to be one of the finest in Ireland. It was built by William Hull in 1818, altered by William Telford in 1854 and further rebuilt by Harrison and Harrison.

During the 1987 restoration some of the original building was revealed, like the outer arch on the east wall which is the extent of the 13th century window. The three niches held the carvings of the three saints, Patrick, Brigid and Columcille in Medieval times.

The font is a massive piece of granite discovered in English Street and probably the base of a Celtic cross from the 10th or 11th centuries. Two fragments of early sculptures, both from the Early Christian period, show a bishop holding a crozier and gospel book and another wearing a rationale, a heavily jewelled ornament worn by bishops of the Celtic church.

CATHEDRAL CHURCH OF CHRIST THE REDEEMER DROMORE

t Colman of Dromore built a church on this ancient Christian site in 510AD, probably thatched using reeds from the River Lagan flowing beside it. In the 12th century King Henry II revised the system of dioceses throughout Ireland and Dromore became the base of the diocese. Little evidence exists of St Colman's church and the medieval church was destroyed in the 1500s. James I in 1609 gave the church the new title and new status of Cathedral Church of the Christ Redeemer but that building was destroyed in 1641 and a new cathedral built by Bishop Jeremy Taylor in 1661.

Exterior stonework reveals the Percy Aisle added in 1811 and a semi-circular sanctuary designed by Thomas Drew during the time of the Reverend Beresford Knox in 1817. The church was made rectangular by the addition of the Harding Aisle in 1899. The existing tower was built in 1808 and the tower porch contains the oak poor man's box and a disused font from 1660.

When a bible was given to the cathedral in 1613 it disappeared during the troubles of 1641, but then reappeared in a shop in County Durham in the 19th century and was finally returned to the cathedral. The bible is bound in oak and leather and can be seen displayed in a case together with other important documents.

The Saurin Pulpit is named after Bishop Saurin, 1760-1842, and is built of Caen stone. It is in an unusual location, facing at right angles to the main aisle, much further down the church than is usual.

The chancel with the bishop's throne and the Latin titles above the stalls relate to the Bishop, Dean, Archdeacon, Chancellor, Presentor, Treasurer and Prebendary. Wooden reliefs on the misericords portray scenes from the lives of those commemorated. The chancel was built in 1870 in memory of Bishop Jeremy Taylor, who is buried with three other bishops below the Sanctuary. The organ, dated from 1871, was installed by Conacher of Huddersfield. For many years early in the 20th century a man received an annual fee for operating the hand bellows through a narrow door on the left.

A tapestry, complementing one in Down, illustrates the parishes of the United Dioceses of Down and Dromore and can be reached by stairs in the porch. The window here depicts the arms of John Meade, first Earl of Clan William, born 1744.

The four central windows in the Harding Aisle, given by the Stott family, are older than the aisle itself since they formed part of the original building before its reconstruction and were only removed by consent of the donors. The marble tablet and memorial window recall the great respect held by the congregation of Dromore for those who served in the First World War.

ST PAUL'S CATHEDRAL DUNDEE

Washed up on the shore near Dundee, victim of a shipwreck near the mouth of the River Tay, the thankful Earl of Huntingdon founded the Church of St Mary and Mary became the Patron Saint of Dundee. The Lady Chapel is dedicated to the Virgin Mary.

St Paul's was built in 1853 for Bishop Forbes who became Bishop of Brechin and promoted the building of the cathedral in Dundee. His vision was for the cathedral to offer refuge to poverty stricken Dundonians then inhabiting unpleasant tenements.

An important feature of the high altar is the mosaic designed by Salviati of Venice. To the left of the altar is the bishop's throne, flanked by carvings on each side of King David holding a model of Brecon Cathedral which he founded, St Andrew the Patron Saint of Scotland, St Paul to whom this cathedral is dedicated and St Modwenna a former abbess of a religious house in Carse of Gowrie.

The font is traditionally found at the entrance to a church so that in early times adults could be baptised before entering the church. The font at St Paul's was discovered in a garden in Newburgh, Fife but came originally from Lindores Abbey in Fife.

Further relics from this abbey are built into the Lindores Cabinet at the north end of the cathedral. For a time they were part of the church's pulpit until Provost Don had the medieval panels built in to a cabinet. There is also a bust of the Provost (1921-31) who went on to become Dean of Westminster Abbey.

St Roque's Chapel is dedicated to the 14th century Italian hero Roque or Roche, Patron Saint of plague victims. Originally St Roque's Church stood in the Blackscroft area of Dundee but in 1950 the congregation of St Roque's merged with St Paul's and the altar and war memorial were moved to the cathedral. There are several commemorative plaques positioned in the Lady Chapel and a portrait of Bishop Forbes. One in particular, the Chalmers' Plaque relates to James Chalmers a local person who invented the adhesive postage stamp but who was never given proper credit for his idea.

The stained glass windows were designed and made by Hardman and Company of Birmingham, the cost borne by anonymous donors. The organ, constructed by Hill and Son in the year the cathedral was consecrated in 1865, was overhauled extensively and reconstructed where necessary in 1975, the work undertaken by Hill, Norman and Beard.

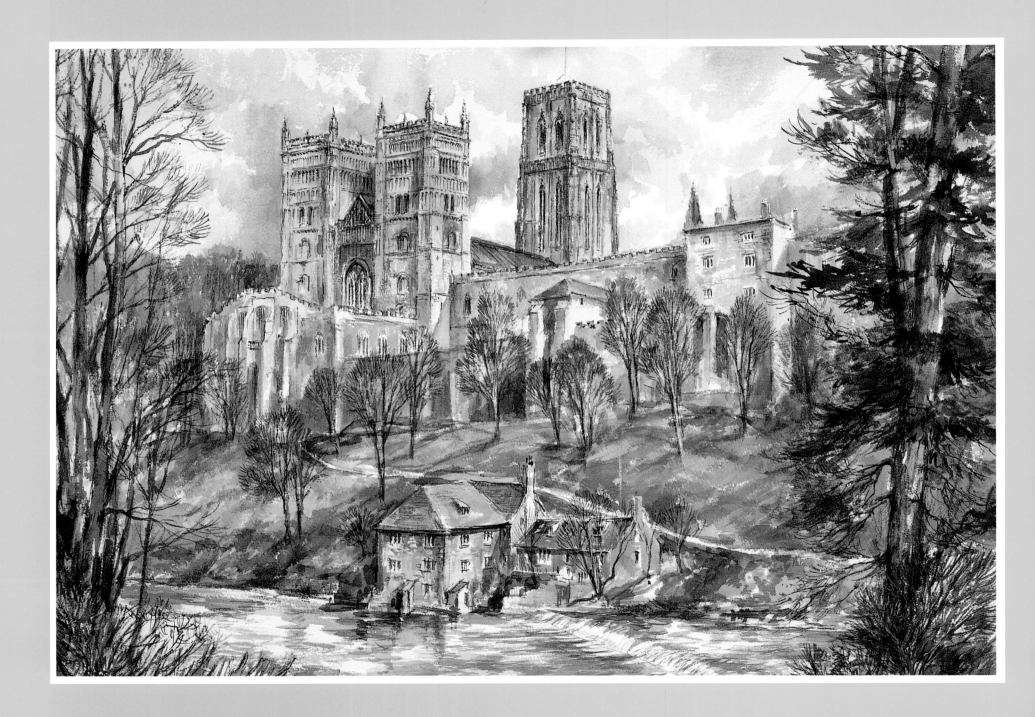

CATHEDRAL CHURCH OF CHRIST AND
THE BLESSED MARY THE VIRGIN - DURHAM

 verlooking the River Wear, Durham combines cathedral, castle and palace and demonstrates the Normans at their most expansive and audacious.

Sent into exile in France for 3 years after quarrelling with King Rufus in 1088, the Bishop of Durham, William of St Calais, was to see the scale of the latest abbey-churches and cathedrals in Normandy and the Isle de France.

He returned, intent on a new, larger cathedral, demolished the Saxon church and 40 years later, in 1133, Durham boasted a unique place of worship, acknowledged as the finest example of early Norman architecture in England.

The building had continued and by 1104 the South and North Transepts were complete. After the death of Bishop Flambard in 1128, the cathedral had no bishop for five years, but the monks took on the responsibility and finished the nave, aisles and stone vaulting.

Originally the Durham Peninsula was the final resting place of Saint Cuthbert, the most prominent saint in the North of England, after his company had carried his coffin around the region to escape marauding Danes. They had erected a small Saxon cathedral, but it was the Normans who later would install a Benedictine Priory.

Another monastic relic of great significance is the remains of the Venerable Bede, who preferred working on his "The Church History of the English People" to becoming abbot of his monastery in Jarrow.

By the time of its consecration in 1130, the cathedral had been substantially completed; the only significant additions being the Galilee Chapel later the same century and the Chapel of the Nine Altars in the 13th century. Records show that the monks kept their church and other buildings in good repair, but the central tower was only finally completed between 1465 and 1490.

A unique record of Durham towards the end of the Middle Ages, written by a monk about monastery life and preserved to this day, first published in 1672, is in a book called the "Rites of Durham".

There were two periods of iconoclasm. The first was in the 16th century when the church was stripped of its furnishings though the main structure remained undamaged. The second followed a century later when 4,000 of Cromwell's Scottish prisoners burnt the medieval wooden furnishings for firewood after the Battle of Dunbar.

By 1777 urgent repairs were again required, this time to the cracks in the vaulting and bulging walls. One crack ran the length of the nave, from east to west, the cloister side wall was bulging outward and stonework everywhere was eroded enough to let water in.

In 1840, some alterations were introduced, principally the removal of the 17th century organ screen to provide an uninterrupted vista from east to west, and though Gilbert Scott was later to erect a marble and alabaster screen which still stands at the choir entrance, one of the remarkable things about the history of Durham Cathedral taken as a whole is how little has been altered.

CATHEDRAL CHURCH OF ST MARY
EDINBURGH

When the Episcopal church was released from the penal laws in 1792 people began thinking about a purpose-built cathedral, and many years later a design was selected after an architectural competition. It was awarded to Gilbert Scott who, drawing inspiration from Ancient Scottish cathedrals and abbeys, went on to design a building some consider his finest work.

The foundation stone was laid on May 21 1874 by the Duke of Buccleuch and Queensbury, whose family remained loyal to the Episcopi for over 100 years. The cathedral is built in stone from the Craigleith quarry and is 80 metres long.

The spire gave Oldrid, a structural engineer, and his father Scott great concern. Edinburgh's strong winds and lack of rock foundations resulted in a complex foundation system going 18 metres deep, combined with flying buttresses. These support four piers that in turn take the load of 6,000 tonnes of principal spire.

The cathedral was consecrated in 1879 and a memorial to Bishop Cotterill, who performed the service, takes the form of three figures over the West Door and represents William of Wickham, Philip the Deacon and Richard of Wallingford a 14th century astronomer. The richly carved tympanum is surrounded by an inscription "I am the door anyone who enters through me shall be saved". Griffins and mythical beasts surround the palisters and the armorial bearings in the clerestory windows are those of the

families that remained loyal to the Episcopal church during the persecution years of 1715 and 1792.

Originally dedicated to All Souls the Chapel was renamed King Charles's Chapel in memory of King Charles I, founder of the diocese of Edinburgh. Amongst the symbolic images on the encaustic tiles are the lion, the fish and the deer, the latter referring to the Drumsheugh estates on which the cathedral now stands, originally part of King David's hunting forest.

The paintings on display in the north aisle include "*Presence*" by Captain A E Borthwick representing a service at the high altar. This was sent to Munich in 1914 for reproductions to be made, and not surprisingly it vanished. After the War it reappeared in an American newspaper and was recognised, and by special Act of Congress it was prevented from being sold as confiscated German property and in due course was returned to the artist who presented it to the cathedral in 1944.

The choir school and St Mary's Music School has a great reputation. The founding of the Edinburgh Festival incorporates many events within the cathedral. A highlight during 1968 was a performance of Benjamin Britten's Three Church Canticles, the Prodigal Son, Curlew River and the Burning Fiery Furnace with Peter Pears in the lead role.

Amongst the relics of past conflicts are the flags of the Battle of Culloden.

CATHEDRAL CHURCH OF THE HOLY AND UNDIVIDED TRINITY - ELY

Looking out over the Fens on a slightly elevated mound, Ely Cathedral is a spectacular sight not far from the river. The old houses in the Close are of great character and it is altogether exceptional in its architecture. Etheldreda, a princess of East Anglia, founded a religious house in 673AD on her land which incorporated the site of the present cathedral and she assigned the principality of the Isle of Ely to the new abbey.

100 years later the Danes destroyed the building and put the religious to the sword, but some escaped and eventually returned to repair the Saxon church. Benedictine monks were introduced and the proprietorship of the area was confirmed by Royal Charter and the Abbey became one of the most opulent of the Middle Ages.

The construction of the present cathedral began with Abbot Simeon prompted by the Benedictines' need for more magnificent churches for their worship. The ambitious scheme continued but work was suspended during the reign of Rufus. The eastern section was finished by 1106 and building continued through the 12th century. The west front and the notable galilee porch of the presbytery were added by Bishop de Northwold in the mid 13th century.

On the night of February 12 1322 the central tower collapsed. Through the initiative of Alan de Walsingham the later Prior of the monastery, an opportunity was taken to widen

both the space and the crossing. Master mason and master carpenter, with great imagination and daring, created the octagon of stone with the lantern extending above constructed of wood faced with lead. The giant oak beams, about 63ft long and 3ft thick, came from Chicksands in Bedfordshire. Roads and bridges near Ely had to be strengthened to take their enormous weight. The octagon remains the most original and daring architectural concept of the Middle Ages.

In the centre of the lantern vaulting is a boss carved in fine detail by John of Burwell who charged two shillings and his keep for executing the work. Etheldreda's shrine was destroyed during the dissolution of the monasteries by orders from Bishop Goodrich, Bishop of Ely, who would become Lord Chancellor of England. With his loyalty to the King destruction continued so that, on this rare occasion, Oliver Cromwell can be exonerated from this particular vandalism. Cromwell himself lived very near to the cathedral in a half-timbered building, now known as Cromwell's House.

Fragments of the monastic buildings still remain, incorporated in houses and schools. The 14th century cele chapel of Prior Crauden is still intact and has become the King's School Chapel. It was here in Ely that Hereward the Wake sought refuge with the monks. Abbot Simeon, a kinsman of William I, saved the monastery by arranging the surrender of Hereward.

CATHEDRAL CHURCH OF ST MACARTIN
ENNISKILLEN

In 1921 the Parish Church of St Anne's became, by consent, the General Synod of the Church of Ireland, the Cathedral of St Macartin. Captain William Cole was mainly responsible for the development of the new town of Enniskillen from 1611. The first building on this site dates from about 1627. Very little remains of the original building but parts of the tower and a small three light window with the date 1637 carved in the stonework is incorporated in the building.

By the beginning of the 19th century the church was not large enough for the expanding population, added to which the spire was unsafe. Therefore, a complete re-building was undertaken and apart from an enlargement to the chancel, the church remains very much as we see it today.

During the 20th century, further expansion has taken place in the Parish of Eniskillen and it became the largest in the Diocese of Clogher. The Diocese is unique in Ireland as it has two cathedrals. In 1995 it was considered time to redecorate the interior and the cathedral was closed from 31 December and planned to re-open on St Patrick's Day in 1996. Unfortunately fire broke out on the 5 March, during the almost complete refurbishment. Although the area affected by the fire was quite small the smoke and water from the hoses did massive damage and the cathedral finally opened during 1997.

Dr Thomas Romney Robertson was Rector from 1821 to 1825. He became a Fellow of the Royal Society and gave up the living to become an astronomer at the observatory in Armagh and produced several publications and scientific treatises. Amongst other notable clergy was William Connor Magee. On leaving this parish he became Dean of Cork, then the Bishop of Peterborough and was consecrated the Archbishop of York where he lies buried.

John Charles Maude was a very long serving rector 1825-1860. The present church was built during his incumbency and he generously gave a new bell to complete the peal of eight. Campanologists are somewhat restricted in their ability to practice their craft in Northern Ireland as less than a dozen churches have eight or more bells. The oak framed housing for the bells at St Macartins was replaced in 1936 by modern steel frames.

Enniskillen is the only town in the British Isles to raise two regiments bearing the town's name, the Royal Enniskillen Fusiliers and the Royal Enniskillen Dragoon Guards. They have ceased to exist as separate regiments and are now combined with other regiments. The two regimental colours can be seen in the Regimental Chapel and a Book of Remembrance records all ranks killed since the Battle of Waterloo. Two stained glass windows act as a further memorial to the two regiments.

The Pokrich stone is mounted in the wall of the church having been discovered when excavating the graveyard during re-building. William Pokrich died in 1628, son of one of the founders of the town and an inscription beside the memorial is a quotation from the last words of Thomas Cromwell, Earl of Essex, beheaded in 1540.

CATHEDRAL CHURCH OF ST PETER
EXETER

In a beautiful setting, Exeter Cathedral stands on what was the site of a Roman town, where King Athelstan, 925-939, commanded that a monastery be built, bestowing his own collection of holy relics and 26 estates. The Minster continued into the late 10th century.

In 1003 Exeter was attacked and burned by the Danes under Sweyn, and the ancient Royal Charters destroyed. Bishop Leofric, whose jurisdiction covered Devon and Cornwall and who was installed by a personal visit by King Edward the Confessor and his Queen, decided to rebuild the Exeter Minster from its run-down condition to become the religious centre of the region.

There is only a small hint of the surviving decoration of the Romanesque cathedral, which would have been a blaze of colour. A small curved stone decorated with birds was discovered in 1942, presumably part of a column used in part of the reconstruction.

William Warelwast, third Bishop of Exeter, nephew of the Conqueror, began the building of the new cathedral of St Peter on the present site leading to consecration in 1258. Work was not finished however, because Walter Bronescombe, the then Bishop of Exeter, felt the existing structure, though new, was inadequate and began a massive reconstruction programme.

The stone quarries used for the construction of the medieval building include those in Beer, Branscombe and Salcombe, Purbeck in Dorset and Caen in Normandy. Some glass was imported from Rouen and lead from Boston in Lincolnshire.

Exeter records reveal that even the most skilled masons were subject to arrest and imprisonment if they attempted to break an engagement before the completion of a particular project. Master masons came from distant places, but the majority of men employed remained in local districts handling the local stone with which they were familiar.

The main work, completed by about 1350, was followed by additions which included the four-sided cloister to the south of the nave with a library above, and the rebuilding of the Chapter House after fire damage. With the Reformation, mural paintings were lime washed, stone altars demolished and images destroyed. The cathedral acquired a font and organ case.

During the bombing of Exeter during the last war, the cathedral suffered a direct hit as much of the ancient town of Exeter was destroyed in the Blitz.

On the morning of 4 May 1942 during a heavy air raid, a large high-explosive bomb exploded in the Chapel of St James in the south quire aisle. Three bays of the aisle and two flying buttresses were destroyed. It also damaged the rear portion of the Bishop's Palace. Mr Herbert Reid the Exeter designer and craftsman was made responsible for assembling trusted craftsmen and volunteer helpers to sort through the fragments of glass and restored the building to its former glory.

ST MARY'S CATHEDRAL
GLASGOW

Architect of the Gothic revival and the man responsible for restoration of London's Albert Memorial, Sir George Gilbert Scott designed St Mary's. The roots of the cathedral stem from the late medieval collegiate church of St Mary which stood by the Tron in the city centre. The penal laws enforced for most of the 18th century restricted the size of congregations at Episcopal services with heavy penalties for any clergy or laity found breaking them. When the laws were repealed in 1792 the Episcopalians could consider fixed places of worship.

The new church of St Mary was consecrated in 1884 and became a vigorous centre for missionary activity and five new churches were established by 1900. The diocese therefore agreed that St Mary's should become a cathedral in 1908.

On the exterior of the cathedral at the base of the tower are statues of Bishop Jocelyn founder of Glasgow's Medieval cathedral, Bishop Turnbull founder of Glasgow University, Archbishop Leighton a Christian leader at the time of Charles II and Bishop Trower seen holding a model of St Mary's in a traditional manner. Erosion has caused some lack of definition on these figures.

The spire is 206 feet high, built by John Oldrid Scott to his father's design in 1893. In the niches of the spireletts are statues of St Andrew, St Mungo, St Margaret Queen of Scotland and St George. A peal of ten bells was hung in the tower in 1907, the tenor bell weighing 32.5 hundredweights.

The five-bay nave is 100 foot long with alternating octagonal and clustered pillars of Bath stone. Above the pillars are carvings of various British saints. The murals, the paintings in the ceiling and the whole decorative scheme is the work of American born artist Gwyneth Leech, who has now returned to the USA to take up a post at the University of Pennsylvania. Behind the nave altar is a notable wrought iron screen designed in 1894 by J.O. Scott.

In 1903 the font was raised on the marble steps and a carved oak canopy, also designed by Scott, was added. The window behind appropriately relates to the sacrament of baptism.

Two large transept windows, depicting the prophets St John the Baptist, Jonah, Isaiah and Ezekiel, are a memorial to Sir George Campbell of Garscube, whose family played an important role in the history of St Mary's. The finest stained glass in the cathedral is the great west window, depicting the history of the foundation of the church.

St Mary's is currently undergoing major restoration. This includes transforming the crossing and chancel, renewing the roof, rebuilding the organ and refurbishing the synod hall.

CATHEDRAL CHURCH OF ST PETER AND THE HOLY AND INDIVISIBLE TRINITY GLOUCESTER

The bishops and dean of Gloucester have been responsible for their cathedral since 1541 when the diocese was formed. The old Benedictine Abbey was surrendered to Henry VIII's commissioners and the Abbey church became Gloucester Cathedral. The ownership of a cathedral is vested in the dean and chapter at the Reformation.

The first bishop inherited a building which had been custom-built for the needs of a monastic community. No less than 15 altars, all in daily use and a Great Cloister which is among the finest in Europe.

The Cloister, completed in 1412, is the work of Abbots Horton and Froucester, who laid the foundation for the high standard of preservation today. Unusually it not only has glassed windows, it uses a revolutionary new type of vaulting, a series of inverted half cones which spread like a fan and are made of Cotswold limestone, the whole effect mirrored in miniature in the monks' lavatorium. In the south walk there are 20 study recesses, all well preserved.

The glory of Gloucester is the Great East Window, the largest and finest surviving medieval stained glass window in England.

The heart of the present building is the Norman Abbey church begun in 1089 and completed around 1126. While most of the Norman work in the nave has survived, the south aisle is 'decorated' in style replacing the Norman aisle which fell down. The rest of the cathedral is perpendicular, some of which is built over the Norman foundations.

Dining at the Abbey in the early 14th century, King Edward II asked if his portrait could join the set of earlier English kings on the walls, to which Abbot Thokey replied that he hoped the King 'would be in a more honourable place'.

His wish was granted, but not in quite the way he had supposed. In 1327 he was murdered in Berkeley Castle by followers of his queen and his body brought finally to Gloucester. A few years later his son had the tomb (which is still in place) embellished with a fine alabaster effigy and covered with a three-pinnacled stone canopy.

The 225ft tower containing England's one surviving great bell of the Middle Ages, built on the Norman foundation in the 15th century and topped with parapet and pinnacles, is a confident expression of the power of the Perpendicular style. The choir, transformed by an architectural genius following the burial of Edward II, is another fine example of the Perpendicular.

The 20th century glass in the Lady Chapel, some of the finest 'Arts and Crafts' work in the country, is by Christopher Whall. Among the memorials are the standing figure of Edward Jenner, the Gloucestershire man who invented a smallpox vaccine, the bust of prison reformer Sir George Onesiphorous Paul, and a large monument to Sarah Morley who in 1784 died at sea returning from India. Three angels receive her and her baby from the rolling waves.

CATHEDRAL CHURCH OF THE HOLY SPIRIT GUILDFORD

Henry VIII nominated Guildford for a Bishopric but it was not until the diocese of Guildford was founded in 1927 that it qualified for cathedral status. With its population increasing the diocese of Winchester was forced to form an independent See and with a national competition for an architect, the successful design for the cathedral was awarded to Sir Edward Maufe. Bishop George Reindorp consecrated the cathedral in 1961 in the presence of HM Queen Elizabeth II and the Duke of Edinburgh.

Work began on the building in 1936 on the site of Stag Hill. Once the hunting ground of Norman kings and centuries later a virgin site commanding wonderful views of the Surrey countryside. A brass stag set in the paving marks the original summit of Stag Hill. Brick on the outside, stone and plaster within, it is built with clay dug from the hill itself. 778 concrete piles were driven 15 metres into the hill to support the building, and local brickyards like Crondall helped to manufacture bricks for the construction of the new cathedral. By paying 2s 6d for a brick, those interested in the project could sign their signature in wet clay and have this fired and built into the cathedral for posterity. This proved a successful way of raising funds.

The roof is reinforced concrete covered with copper and Maufe used limestone from Doulting in Somerset for the interior. The nave floor is of travertine marble from Italy. Guildford is a simplified version of a medieval church. The towers are similar to that of the Merchant Taylor's School by Scott, one of Maufe's mentors. External sculpture was designed by Eric Gill but completed after his death. The angel on the tower is the work of John Skeaping RA and inside is a bronze portrait of Maufe by his close friend Sir Charles Wheeler, former President of the Royal Academy and well known for his fountains in Trafalgar Square.

The small round window at the east end is symbolic of the Holy Spirit to which the cathedral is dedicated. The 1,460 kneelers are all handmade and are a unique feature. The Bishop's Throne is situated under a carved, guilded canopy and the blue woven backing features an embroidered dove descending. Beyond the altar rails is the handmade Wilton carpet designed by Maufe, illustrating the arms of the diocese, supported by decorative angels.

The Children's Chapel is a place of pilgrimage where bereaved parents may seek spiritual rest. Cast in the foundry at Whitechapel, the twelve bells are rung regularly and the Choir has gained a reputation through regular broadcasts on the BBC and they have also recorded many high-quality choral works.

CATHEDRAL CHURCH OF THE BLESSED VIRGIN MARY AND ST ETHELBERT - HEREFORD

The Cathedral Church of St Mary and St Ethelbert is set in an agricultural region near the Black Mountains of Wales. Originally a Saxon Church built under the direction of Bishop Athelstan, it was destroyed by the Welsh in the 11th century and replaced by a Norman cathedral. Today the Saxon font is all that remains of the original church.

Friend of Simon de Montfort, Thomas de Cantilupe, one of the most popular prelates of the 13th century and a former Grand Master of the Knights Templar, was a scholarly bishop and created much of the wealth of Hereford. Canonised by the Pope in 1320, this saint attracted many pilgrims to the city and along with it money to the area. An elaborate shrine was erected to St Cantilupe, which was later destroyed.

Today, much of Hereford is Victorian. The quire floor, the pew ends, the high altar reredos, the replica Norman arch - all were restored in the 19th century by scholarship and skill which rescued the cathedral from terminal decline.

Dating from about 1290 the Mappa Mundi is the centrepiece of the great collection of Medieval books and maps in the award winning Chained Library. The library has a wonderful collection of manuscripts and early printed books on a wide range of subjects, including the 8th century Hereford Gospels and the Hereford Breviary containing dedications to St Ethelbert.

The diocese of Hereford has a twinning arrangement with the Lutheran Christians of Nuremburg and the fine German altar piece is a gift expressing this link. The Bishop's throne is incorporated in the choir stalls which are enriched with original canopies and beautifully carved misericords. A statue of St Ethelbert, the cathedral's patron, stands to the right of the High Altar. As King of East Anglia, he was murdered by the order of King Offa in 794AD. St Ethelbert is considered a martyr saint and his shrine attracted large numbers of Pilgrims in the Middle Ages.

Other saints drew pilgrims to Hereford. Still in the cathedral's possession is a small reliquary, made in Limoges, containing a relic of St Thomas Becket and in 1220 Archbishop Stephen Langton of Canterbury marked Becket's 50th anniversary by preaching at Hereford.

Amongst the many treasures of Hereford there is a fine processional cross, literally walled up during the reformation and rediscovered in the 19th century, which dates from about 1350. The Crypt dates from 1225, the simplicity of expression of early English architecture is acknowledged to be one of the finest in the country.

ST ANDREWS CATHEDRAL
INVERNESS

The cathedral is situated in an attractive setting by the River Ness. The Reformation was a great upheaval in Scotland. In 1560 the Scots Parliament abolished paper authority and forbade Latin mass, but there were varying opinions within the Scottish church as to the degree of reform. Episcopalian and Presbyterian struggled with each other to gain dominance.

The final separation centred on political friction created when James II fled to France and William of Orange was offered the crown. The established Church of Scotland then became Presbyterian. Episcopalian clergy were banned from public life, ecclesiastical ministrations and many were ejected from their manses.

After the Jacobite rising of 1715 even more stringent laws were passed on the Episcopal Church. Soldiers set parsonages on fire and the following years marked a great decline.

The election of Robert Eden in 1851 as Bishop of Moray and Ross was a turning point. He had a vision of a cathedral in Inverness and consequently moved there in 1853. The congregation agreed to the bishop's proposal to build the cathedral on 17 January 1866 and Alexander Ross the architect was commissioned to prepare designs. The foundation stone was laid by Dr Charles Longley, Archbishop of Canterbury, in October 1866, the first official act by an English Primate since Presbyterianism was established.

The cathedral cost £15,106. When it was opened a debt of £6,835 remained and since a church cannot be consecrated until all debts are settled the congregation set about fundraising and cleared the debt within 5 years, a remarkable achievement, and so the first cathedral completed since the Reformation was consecrated on 29 September 1874.

The inaugural sermons by Samuel Wilberforce, Bishop of Oxford and the Bishop of Rochester indicate the high regard held for Bishop Eden. Educated at Winchester and Christ Church Oxford, he was great uncle to Sir Anthony Eden, the British Prime Minister.

The cathedral was built in sandstone from Conon and from Covsea near Elgin, with an overall length of 50 metres and a design adapted from the original containing two spires. The ninth bell in the north tower was presented by the Provost and citizens of the burgh as a mark of esteem for the vision and committed work of Bishop Eden.

The carving of a horse on the transept window overlooking the river tells us of a legend that the horse operating the hoist to raise masonry during the cathedral's construction was killed in an accident. Above the doorway of the impressive front of the cathedral is a sculpture by Thomas Earp (1875) of Christ's Missionary Commission to the Apostles. Other statues also form part of the entrance design and are of John the Baptist and Saints Andrew, Paul and Peter.

CATHEDRAL CHURCH OF ST MARTIN
LEICESTER

The Cathedral is built on the site of a Roman temple, just as modern Leicester lies above the old Roman town of Ratae. St Martin was a Roman soldier who left the army to become a monk, later to be elevated to the position of the Bishop of Tours in France. After his death in 397AD his name was adopted as the patron saint of Leicestershire.

Cuthwine became the first Saxon Bishop in 680AD. In 870 the whole Midlands area was invaded and occupied by the Danes, the last Saxon Bishop fled and Leicester ceased to be an independent diocese. In 1072 the Normans placed Leicester under the jurisdiction of first, the Lincoln diocese and later the Peterborough one. It was not until 1927 that Leicester again had its own bishop and St Martin's Church became his cathedral.

Nine hundred years ago, the Normans began to build today's structure. It was rebuilt and enlarged in the 13th and 15th centuries and developed strong links with the merchants and guilds of Leicester.

In 1535 the nearby Greyfriars Monastery closed down and in 1548 the Reformation saw great destruction of sculpture, screens, stained glass and many artefacts of St Martin's. The church received two important Royal visits - these were made by King Charles I in 1634 and 1642.

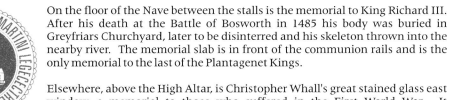

The Victorian restoration began in 1860 with rebuilding of the tower and roof under the direction of Raphael Brandon. A new 220ft spire was added and although the cathedral can now be difficult to find in a maze of narrow streets, the spire has become the focal point of the area. Above the south door the Vaughan porch was built by J L Pearson, architect of Truro Cathedral, as a memorial to the four Vaughans who were Parish priests here during the 19th century.

On the floor of the Nave between the stalls is the memorial to King Richard III. After his death at the Battle of Bosworth in 1485 his body was buried in Greyfriars Churchyard, later to be disinterred and his skeleton thrown into the nearby river. The memorial slab is in front of the communion rails and is the only memorial to the last of the Plantagenet Kings.

Elsewhere, above the High Altar, is Christopher Whall's great stained glass east window, a memorial to those who suffered in the First World War. It symbolises the power that rules the universe and the hope for peace.

On the north side is St Katharine's Chapel, restored in memory of the 17th century poet Robert Herrick. For centuries the Herrick family provided mayors, town clerks and clergy for Leicester. Another chapel, St Dunstan's, caters specifically for the prayers of local people.

CATHEDRAL CHURCH OF THE BLESSED VIRGIN MARY AND ST CHAD - LICHFIELD

Lichfield is unique in the architecture of English cathedrals, being the only cathedral to have three sandstone spires, known as the "Ladies of the Vale". Most of the present Gothic building dates from the 13th century, although the cathedral suffered extensive damage in the Civil War.

Visitors have been welcomed for 1,300 years, ever since the first cathedral was founded in honour of St Chad and dedicated to St Peter in 700. The earlier Saxon church dedicated to St Mary was probably built on the "field of the dead" where Christians were martyred by the Romans.

St Chad was to have three resting places. From his Saxon shrine he was moved to the choir of the new Norman cathedral begun in 1085 and developed in the 12th century, and finally after its destruction in 1541, a modern shrine now graces today's Lady Chapel.

Medieval pilgrims arriving to see the beautiful new cathedral would find 113 painted and gilded statues on the west front, St Chad among them seated with Norman and Saxon kings.

These and other treasures were looted and smashed by Roundheads after the Royalists had found the cathedral's gateways and Bishop de Langton's fortifications made a perfect fortress. The extensive damage reduced the building to a shell which was then repaired rather than restored. Medieval stained glass became clear glass and the grand 15th century altar screen made way for a makeshift replacement.

It was architect James Wyatt in the 1790s who began serious restoration work which was

continued in the 1850s by Sir George Gilbert Scott. For half a century, Victorian visitors and worshippers shared their cathedral with scaffolding and building works. Light and colour, absent for over 200 years, flooded back with attractive local stone and, in particular, a newly laid floor of Minton tiles and a new choirscreen by Skidmore. The choir arches were unblocked and the high altar installed again, and by 1900 a cathedral much like the one we see today was reborn.

In 1817 sculptor Sir Francis Chantrey produced "The Sleeping Children" a monument to two young sisters at the end of the south choir aisle, but elsewhere Victorian wood and stone carving is evident in the arcading, in the carved heads and animals of the Chapter House and in the choirstalls.

Above the Chapter House, the library floor retains its original late 13th century tiles, patterns which would later influence a tile-making revival in the 1800s. Another good example of fine tilework is in the memorial in the Lady Chapel to Bishop Selwyn, Bishop of Lichfield 1867-78.

There is one large hidden treasure, an organ which boasts 4,000 pipes and one of 10 bells weighing more than 1½ tonnes. The bells were given by the Freemasons of Staffordshire to commemorate the 750th anniversary of the cathedral. Within the shadow of the cathedral lived Erasmus Darwin, grandfather of Charles.

As Lichfield enters the 21st century, it looks forward to further establishing its links, through the Diocese, to the Anglican Church in Canada and Malaysia and the Lutheran Church in Germany.

CATHEDRAL CHURCH OF THE BLESSED VIRGIN MARY LINCOLN

The first Norman bishop of Lincoln was Remigius, a Benedictine monk and supporter of William the Conqueror at Hastings, whose diocese was the largest in England, stretching from London to the Humber. William moved the bishopric to London in 1072 as this was the major city in the diocese with a Royal castle already well established. Remigius did not live to see his cathedral completed and it was consecrated in May 1092.

It is assumed that the cathedral was damaged by fire during the Civil War between King Stephen and his cousin Matilda in 1141, but it was rebuilt and restored by Alexander, Bishop of Lincoln 1123-1148, who travelled extensively, acquainting himself with the most advanced architecture of his time.

During the time of Bishop St Hugh 1186-1200, a Carthusian monk from Avalon, an earthquake was recorded and major structural damage occurred. The west front of the cathedral was retained and rebuilding commenced in the Gothic style in 1192, to include flying buttresses which allowed for a more delicate construction with a much larger window area for stained glass.

However, such experimental techniques were new and when the central tower collapsed about 1237, a replacement tower was started immediately and permission was obtained from Henry III to demolish part of the town wall to enlarge the building. Expansion was partly necessary to cope with the growing number of pilgrims venerating the shrine of St Hugh.

All three towers had spires until the central spire blew down in 1548. Architect James Gibbs added strengthening cross walls but it was necessary to remove the western spires in 1807 as they were considered unsafe. The only part remaining of the original cathedral is the central section of the west front. The 13th century Gothic screen today is surmounted by a statue of St Hugh and the Romanesque frieze commissioned by Bishop Alexander contains many delightful sculpture panels including Adam and Cain and the Birth of Abel. Today's sculptors are conserving and restoring some of these panels and replacing excellent work in the Romanesque style.

The stained glass windows suffered at the hands of 16th century reformers and 17th century parliamentarians and apart from small fragments of glass in the nave the stained glass is Victorian but of fine quality. The Sutton brothers were responsible for the Great West Window and the Rose Window above depicts Bishop Remigius holding a miniature of the church design. The window was commissioned by Charles Tennyson d'Eyncort, uncle of Alfred Lord Tennyson. A life size bronze of the poet by G F Watts stands in the cathedral grounds.

Katherine Swynford, the second wife of John of Gaunt, Duke of Lancaster and Earl of Lincoln is buried in the chantry chapel. They were married in Lincoln Cathedral. The Russell Chantry, a late Gothic annex, contains the tomb of Bishop John Russell, Lord Chancellor to Richard III. The wall paintings here date from 1958 and are by Duncan Grant.

CATHEDRAL CHRIST CHURCH LISBURN

Early in the 17th century a Welsh officer in the English army settled in Lisnagarvey in the territory of Killultagh. He built a castle and in 1623 constructed a church dedicated to St Thomas, this was on the site of the present cathedral. Little is known of the original building but the settlement grew in Lisnagarvey as the district was then called but in 1641 the town was attacked by a rebel army and the church destroyed. Civil conflict continued but not in Lisburn, the new name, enabling the church to be rebuilt and reconstructed.

In 1662 the church of Lisburn was granted a charter of cathedral status by Charles II. The transmiss of the charter is preserved in the public records office in Belfast, an extract follows:

"And whereas the Church of Lisburne alias Lisnagarvie, in the country of Antrim and Diocese of Down, being situate near the middle of the dioceses aforesaid, and now united, can more conveniently serve for a Cathedral Church for the bishopricks aforesaid, we ..... have erected, created, founded, ordained, made, constituted and established the said church of Lisburne, alias Lisnagarvie, and place of the same Church to be for ever hereafter the Episcopal seat of the aforesaid several bishopricks of Down and Connor and to continue for ever in all future times"

As the document had never been approved by Parliament some doubt was raised as to its validity. In order to remove all doubt Bishop Charles King Irwin introduced a Bill at the General Synod of the Church of Ireland in 1952 to dispel all doubts. The measure recognised Lisburn as the Cathedral of the Diocese of Connor, known as the Cathedral of Christ Church Lisburn.

The church was reconstructed in 1674 and it was noted as being in good repair by the arrival of Huguenot families who established their own church in Castle Street, although several members were later buried in the cathedral churchyard.

The castle, town and church were destroyed by a disastrous fire in April 1707 but in 1708, due to enormous efforts, the foundation of a new church was made, this being the third building on this site. Later the clock and bell tower were presented by the Marquis of Hertford, the slim cut stone octagonal tower was built between 1804 and 1807 and is a very prominent landmark in the Lagan Valley.

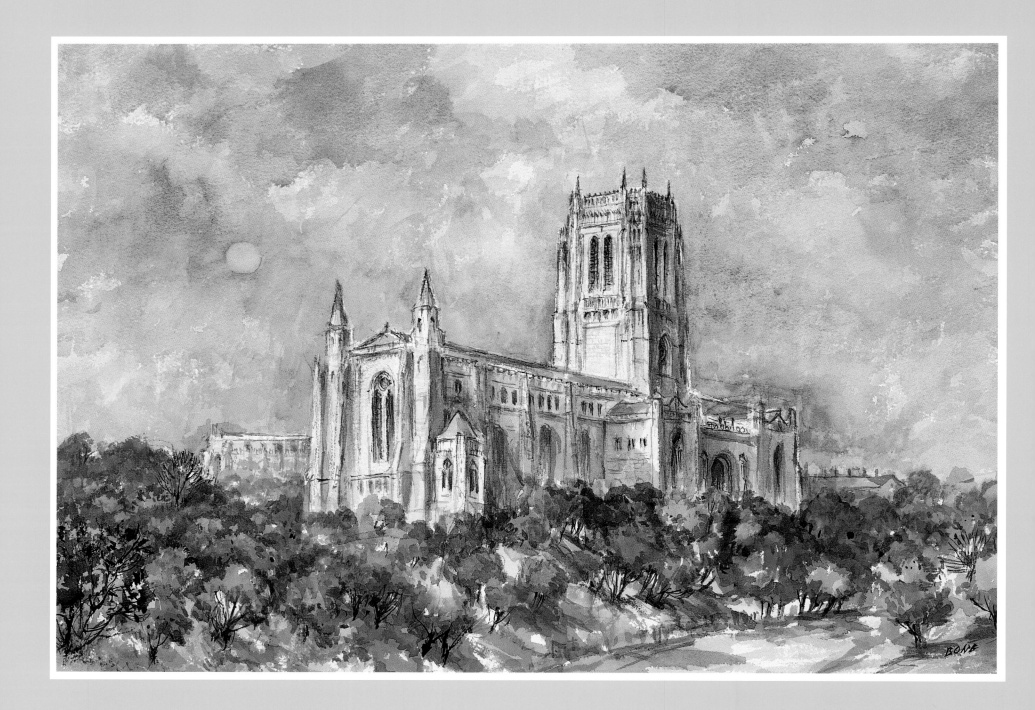

CATHEDRAL CHURCH OF CHRIST LIVERPOOL

The new diocese of Liverpool was formed out of the diocese of Chester in 1890. St Peter's Church was used as a cathedral by the first bishop but the building was not suitable for the expanding population of the city. Bishop Chavasse, the second bishop, formed a committee chaired by the Earl of Derby in 1901 with the purpose of designing a new cathedral and a shortlist of five possible architects was drawn up.

The design of Giles Gilbert Scott was selected. He was a Roman Catholic and was 22 years old at the time and this was a brave decision by the committee. Gilbert Scott's grandfather had achieved much in the restoration of cathedrals and the design of St Pancras Station, so to some extent the large scale work was in his blood. His age may have also proved an asset, like Maufe at Guildford he was able to see the majority of the work through.

Medieval cathedrals had no central heating and no organ as instruments used were string and brass, so for the first time the organ, which in Liverpool is one of the finest in the world is an integral part of the design. The first dean, the Very Reverend F W Dweley planned the consecration service and was responsible for the design of most of the ceremonial robes and furnishings. The cathedral was built over a period of 74 years using local sandstone. At one point 240 craftsmen were employed in the work. It is the largest Anglican cathedral in England and the fifth largest in the world.

Sir Giles Scott died in 1960 but the work continued with Frederick Thomas and Roger Pinkney and the cathedral was finally dedicated in 1978 in the presence of HM Queen Elizabeth II.

The Vestey Tower is so called because of the generosity of the family in financing its construction. It contains the belfry and ringing chamber, the largest bell weighing14.75 tonnes. The font is 12 sided with an apostle carved on each facet and the oak cover, extending twenty metres high, is an echo of medieval design.. The material used is Lunel Rubane a marble from France.

Within the cathedral shop in the south transept is an aerial sculpture, "The Spirit of Liverpool" by Keith Scott, the present architect of the cathedral and sculptor Dame Elisabeth Frink created the bronze figure of the welcoming Christ overlooking the city. The Lady Chapel at the east end was the first completed part of the building and contains a statue by the 15th century sculptor Giovanni della Robbia, famous for his use of colour in ceramic.

A book of remembrance designed by George Scruby and signed by King George V, contains the names of 14,000 servicemen of Liverpool who died in the First World War. Links with the Battle of the Atlantic in the Second World War are symbolised by the bell of HMS Liverpool hanging in the North West Transept. Soldiers of the Kings Own Liverpool Regiment attend Evensong each month as an act of remembrance. In the Memorial Chapel is a bust of Captain Noel Chavasse, son of Bishop Chavasse the only serviceman to be awarded the VC twice in the First World War.

CATHEDRAL CHURCH OF SS PETER AND PAUL WITH SS DYFRIG, TEILO AND EUDDOGWY - LLANDAFF

At the site of the Cathedral in Llandaff there is evidence of pre-Christian burials under the western part of the church. Teilo and two other Celtic bishops were associated with early Christian life in Llandaff and the three mitres on the present arms symbolise these three patron saints. An old well in the Cathedral School grounds is known as Telio's well.

The pre-Norman church, known as the little minster, measuring 28 feet by 15 feet wide stood until the early 12th century. Today, the building has disappeared completely apart from the 10th century Celtic cross.

Urban, the first Norman bishop, began construction of the present building. In order to improve the status of Llandaff the bones of St Dyfrig were moved from Bardsey Island, to be buried instead on the north side of the Sanctuary. From that date St Dyfrig was referred to as the first Bishop of Llandaff.

King John granted Llandaff a four day annual fair at Whitsuntide which continued until the end of the 19th century when Dean Vaughan stopped the event with the celebrations getting out of hand.

With the construction of the muniment room and chapter house a great dedication service was held on the 23 November 1266. At the same time Bishop William de Braose was enthroned. On his death he was buried in the Sanctuary of the Lady Chapel which now contains his effigy.

Medieval Bishop Marshall a benefactor of the cathedral, had a new throne constructed, and though it was destroyed during the 18th century, and escaped destruction during The Civil War by being camouflaged in black lead, the painting on wood which formed the back of the throne has survived. It occupies a permanent position in the Euddogwy Chapel.

Jasper Tudor, uncle of Henry VII, and Duke of Bedford, commissioned the last medieval feature, the north west Tower. It houses ten bells, which were rehung by the 53rd Welsh Infantry Division as a result of the war damage to the housing.

This tower, built 1485-1500, is Llandaff's most distinctive feature, and was designed in the best tradition with a pinnacled coronet.

The cathedral passed through a difficult time in the late 17th century, causing Archdeacon Bull in 1697 to describe it "our sad and miserable Cathedral". Cromwell's troops continued the indignity by turning part into a beer house and part into a post office while the font was used for pig feed and the library burnt.

Following a violent storm in 1723 which destroyed the 13th century south tower, a natural phenomenon deserving of mention in Evelyn's diary, the 18th century restoration work began under John Wood, the architect famous for classical Bath.

In the Illtud Chapel lies the Rossetti triptych, in which Burne Jones, Swinburne and William Morris were the models. Porcelain panels by Burne Jones are in the St Dyfrig's Chapel, the model being Elizabeth Siddal, the inspiration for Swinburne's poems and the great love of Rossetti.

Sir Jacob Epstein's work "Christus" dominates the interior and together with the John Piper window depicting the supper of Emmaus, brings the 20th century religious art into the cathedral.

The south doorway is Norman work of fretted wrought iron which withstood the landmine of 1941 without damage and remains a good reference to the quality of Norman craftsmen.

CATHEDRAL CHURCH OF ST PAUL
LONDON

The first church on this site was built in 600 by Mellitus and was of a wooden structure. This was severely damaged by the Vikings. Later a stone cathedral was constructed by St Erkenwald, a bishop about 680AD. The church in the Middle Ages was one of the largest. Written accounts exist but the clear impression of the scale is illustrated by the engravings of Wencelaus Hollar. It was some 183 metres long with an enormous spire but the old St Paul's was largely destroyed in the Great Fire of London in 1666.

After the Great Fire, Sir Christopher Wren had plans to redesign the City. 15 new churches and the cathedral came into being, largely financed through the tax on coal entering the City ports. The construction of the new cathedral began in 1675 and finished in 1710.

Wren had put forward a scheme before the Great Fire. A large number of stone carvers, the best that could be found were employed. Nathanial Rawlins, Christopher and William Kempster and the exquisite wood carvings of Grinling Gibbons.

Wren ignored medieval tradition and conceived the interior flooded with light. Although revised from the original plan at nearly 80 Wren did see the plans complete.

St Paul's Cathedral sits on an imposing site on Ludgate Hill, a monumental landmark of London and is used for great national occasions. The music of Handel conveys the majestic character of the cathedral.

Monochrome frescos by Sir James Thornhill illustrating the life of St Paul's were illustrated on the inside of the dome. The Duke of Wellington's monument by Alfred Stevens took 20 years to complete and the monument to Nelson is by John Flaxman.

Bombing in the last war in 1940 destroyed parts of the cathedral but the dome remained a symbol to those in the Blitz and a plaque commemorating Sir Winston Churchill's funeral in 1965 is positioned under the dome itself.

Henry Moore, one of the outstanding figures of the century is well represented by his sculpture of a "Mother and Child".

CATHEDRAL AND COLLEGIATE CHURCH OF ST MARY, ST DENYS AND ST GEORGE - MANCHESTER

On the nave wall of this cathedral is a copy of the original Charter for building a new church obtained in May 1421 by Thomas de la Warre from Henry V. The Bishop of Lichfield together with Pope Martin V granted permission to proceed with the building, and a copy of the Pope's document of approval was found in the Vatican. John Huntington, the then Rector of Ashton under Lyne, was appointed the first warden. He is commemorated in a very fine brass over his tomb in the presbytery.

Under Huntington's direction the quire and the aisles were built and Ralph Langley, warden from 1465 to 1485, built the nave. The good work continued with the two James Stanleys, the second of which was the son of the first Earl of Derby, later to become Bishop of Ely. His stepmother was the mother of King Henry VII.

On either side of the nave are double aisles, the outer area used originally as a series of chantry chapels. When, in the last century the partitions were removed to make room for a larger congregation, this created a very wide nave compared to other cathedrals. Winchester is 80 feet, York Minster is 104 feet, Derby 60 but Manchester is 114 feet wide. Two piscina on the walls are the only remains of evidence of the nave chantries. The ancient chapel of Huntington was destroyed by bombs in 1940 and has been replaced by a modern chapel.

The massive oak quire screen divides the cathedral into two parts. It is beautifully carved with tracery and carvings of castles, flowers, birds and animals on the stalls, particularly on those used by the dean and canon. The quality is outstanding and was completed in about 1508 by master craftsmen who also worked in Beverley Minster and Ripon Cathedral. The hinged misericords show great imagination by the carver, a fox teaching two cubs to read, two men playing backgammon.

After the church received its cathedral status in 1847, the Victorians carried out much needed restoration of the stone work. Over the west door of the cathedral is the Victoria Porch designed by Basil Champneys to commemorate Victoria's Diamond Jubilee, featuring a statue of Victoria by her daughter Princess Louise, Duchess of Argyll.

Sculpture in the cathedral ranges from the ancient angel stone that formed part of the tympanum of the ancient Saxon church here to the carving by Eric Gill and over the entrance to the south porch a carving of the Good Shepherd by Alan Durst. The stone tracery over the entrance to the Chapter House has been filled with timber and contains the excellent murals of Professor Carel Weight RA. His bold, romantic style fits in well.

CATHEDRAL OF THE ISLES AND COLLEGIATE CHURCH OF THE HOLY SPIRIT - MILLPORT

The Cathedral of the Isle is probably the smallest in Europe, seating about 70 people with a nave 40 feet by 20 feet. It is part of a complex of attractive ecclesiastical buildings. The Isle of Cumbrae is situated in the Firth of Clyde on the West Coast of Scotland, less than four miles long and two miles wide, with views of Arran and the Argyll and Ayrshire coasts.

Architect William Butterfield was invited by the Hon. George Frederick Boyle to reconstruct buildings in the grounds of his island home to create a private chapel for his mother the Dowager Countess of Glasgow, to be dedicated to St Andrew. The local Episcopalians used this as a place of worship for many years and Butterfield became an important architect of the Gothic revival and amongst his other achievements was Keble College, Oxford. The designs for the Collegiate Foundation included a church, two college buildings, a chapter house, a refectory and cloister, unique buildings which were opened in 1851 together with the first students of theology.

In due course Boyle became the Earl of Glasgow and in 1875 handed over the

buildings to the Trustees of the Scottish Episcopal Church and on May 3rd 1876 the Church was elevated to the status of Cathedral of the Diocese of the Isles and pro Cathedral of Argyll.

Following the financial crash of 1885 the Earl of Glasgow was obliged to sell all his land on Cumbrae and St Andrews was passed to the Marquis of Bute and services were suspended. The cathedral and Collegiate buildings were saved for the Episcopal Church by the generosity of Mrs Chinnery Haldane, wife of the Diocesan Bishop. The College closed in 1886 but reopened 60 years later when a test school was created for the preliminary training of ex-service candidates for Holy Orders.

An entry in the Service Register states Evensong was interrupted by a great storm that blew in the west window of the church. It was the same storm that blew over the Tay railway bridge on Sunday 28th December 1879. The window was replaced with geometric designs as a gift from the workmen who built the cathedral, to express their thanks for surviving its construction.

CATHEDRAL CHURCH OF ST NICHOLAS NEWCASTLE

The bridging of the Tyne by the Romans gave the area importance and made possible the construction of Hadrian's Wall and later the Norman Castle and indeed the town itself. This part of England took on even greater significance when Robert, William the Conqueror's elder son, built a castle here to establish a military foothold in these parts.

Monkchester was the earlier name of Newcastle and it is believed that the first Church of St Nicholas was founded in 1091 by St Osmund, Earl of Dorset and Bishop of Salisbury. This was probably a wooden structure but rebuilt in stone at the end of the 12th century.

In Medieval times churches were used for legal, political and spiritual purposes and the Church of St Nicholas was no exception. A truce between England and Scotland was signed in the vestry in 1451. By the year 1500 there were no less than 18 altars in the church.

The 13 year old Princess Margaret, daughter of Henry VII, attended mass in St Nicholas on her way to marry James IV of Scotland who, ten years later, was killed in the Battle of Flodden.

John Knox preached at St Nicholas in 1550. Although it was suggested he became the first Bishop of St Nicholas the proposed division of the See of Durham by creating a bishopric in Newcastle did not occur until over 300 years later when St Nicholas became a cathedral church.

For seven months Charles I was a virtual prisoner in Newcastle and obliged to listen to sermons aimed at his reform. At one such service, presumed to be at St Nicholas, the minister announced psalm 52 "Why dost thou tyrant boast aloud thy wicked word to praise" The King suggested instead psalm 51 beginning "Have mercy on me Lord I pray".

St Nicholas housed a library of 5,000 books which eventually formed the first public library when removed to what is now the City Library in 1885.

In 1865 the tower was seen to be leaning to the north due to the collapse of early foundations in 1813. Sir Gilbert Scott supervised the underpinning and the north porch was built and the tower buttressed. R T Johnson, a local architect, was commissioned to design the refurnishing of the church in line with its use as a cathedral and on May 17 1882 St Nicholas was elevated to cathedral status.

The 15th century font is one of the main features. The lower section is carved in frosterley marble with eight coats of arms displayed, and the overhanging canopy contains a sculpture of the Coronation of the Virgin. Amongst many important monuments is a bust of Lord Collingwood of Hethpool and Coldburn, the hero of the Battle of Trafalgar.

CATHEDRAL CHURCH OF ST WOOLOS
NEWPORT

Lord of Gwyllwg converted by Tathan of Caerwent, founded the church in 500AD. Little evidence remains of the building but the church still possesses a narrow entrance to St Mary's Chapel, believed to be on the site of the original building. St Woolos was selected as a cathedral because of its great antiquity and its situation at the centre of the diocese. Cas Newydd is the town's Welsh name and the castle ruins still lie on the banks of the River Usk. The present cathedral overlooks the town's harbour and docklands.

In the 15th century the church suffered damage at the hands of Owen Glyndwr but the church was later restored and increased in size by Jasper Tudor, uncle to Henry VII. The south side was heightened and the south porch added with the priest's room above, while the tower and north aisle were also built at this time.

A statue thought to be that of Jasper Tudor is on the outside of the tower. Unfortunately it has lost its head and a leg, probably through weather erosion of the stone, although popularly attributed to musket fire from Cromwell's troops.

Remnants of alabaster monuments are positioned in a niche in the Lady Chapel. One is to the memory of Knight of the Holy Sepulchre, Sir John Morgan of Tredegar and his wife and dates from 1491. The female figure is thought to be the wife of William de Berkerolles, dated 1226, and another armoured figure is thought to be her husband.

Another notable monument is to a former High Sheriff of Monmouthshire Sir Walter Herbert of St Julians. He died in 1568 and his tomb suffered mutilation but it has been restored and cleaned as the result of the generosity of the Friends of the Cathedral and the Pilgrim Trust.

In 1818 St Mary's Chapel was restored, when lancets were widened and an organ built on the singing gallery, but a full restoration took place in 1853 during the incumbency of Canon Hawkins. The chancel was almost completely rebuilt, two medieval windows were uncovered and preserved and the damaged Norman font was rescued, restored and positioned near the porch in the south aisle.

A young architect, R G Thomas, planned to replace the Norman nave with a Gothic one but fortunately this was not carried out, he emigrated to Australia and became a key figure in the country's Gothic revival.

The Victorian chancel was demolished in 1960 and a modern chancel built, the architect was A D R Caroe. The new structure incorporated a small medieval window, known as the leper window. The construction of the mural here was undertaken by scenery painters from the Covent Garden Opera House and, together with the east window, was designed by John Piper.

The bell tower houses a peal of 13 bells, the largest in Wales, which have been slowly developed since 1768 when there were only five.

CATHEDRAL CHURCH OF THE HOLY AND UNDIVIDED TRINITY - NORWICH

The year 630AD marks the final conversion to Christianity of East Anglia. The Burgundian monk Felix's See was at the Suffolk port of Dunwich, now vanished due to coastal erosion. Thirty years after the Norman Conquest Norwich became the seat of East Anglia's bishop. Until then the village of North Elmham, with its small cathedral, had the distinction.

A former monk, Herbert of Losinga, reached agreement with William Rufus and began the building of a Benedictine monastery as his cathedral in Norwich, and in order to carry out the plans part of the town was demolished. Before his death in 1119 the cathedral extended from the east to the altar of the nave and the work was continued by his successor, creating a cathedral 140 metres long. Stone from Caen, light in colour, came by sea and river. During the rebuilding of the Norman Cloister in later years the work was directed by master mason James Woderford, noted for his excellence.

In 1362 the spire collapsed, causing much damage and additional work had to be carried out over the presbytery. The area in East Anglia was at this time growing very wealthy from the cloth trade and farming, expansion reflected in the quality of work in the cathedral.

The reteble, above the altar in the St Luke's Chapel, gives some idea of the achievement of East Anglian artists at this time. This tradition continued through the centuries to the Norwich School of painters. Amongst the heraldic symbols surrounding the five panels are those of Bishop Hugh Despenser who turned the little North Elmham Cathedral into a fortified hunting lodge.

From the East Walk, a prior's door, which originally led to the Chapter House, is extremely beautiful and carved with canopied figures of bishops and saints around the arch. It is possibly the work of John Ramsey, dating from 1305. This has survived although the original Chapter House is gone, destroyed in the reign of Elizabeth I.

In the late 15th century new vaults were built over the nave. 400 bosses enriched the ceiling with carvings of biblical themes, one of which is a highly original version of The Last Supper. Many are based on medieval daily life.

The cathedral suffered, as others did, from the rioters of the 1640s and they caused much havoc. The 15 quire stalls and 52 misericords are still a delight to see but received some damage over their long history.

Nurse Edith Cavell, shot in the First World War, is buried here.

ST JOHN THE DIVINE CATHEDRAL
OBAN

The Episcopal Church has a long history in the West Highlands of Scotland, beginning in Jacobite times. When the congregation of St John the Divine first assembled in 1846, there were Episcopalians from Appin, Ballachulish and Glencoe together with Anglicans from Ireland and England.

Two local lairds, Macdougall of Dunollie and Campbell of Dunstaffnage were heavily involved at the start of the building and the descendants are still connected with the congregation. Charles Wilson was chosen as architect but unfortunately died before the project was completed, and the commission was taken over by David Thomson who completed the middle zone of the cathedral, omitting the tower and spire.

Oban, originally a village surrounded by open fields, became a popular resort but very overcrowded. On the 17 August 1872 the Oban Times reported that Prince Fredrick Charles of Prussia, Count Bismarck and others could not be

accommodated in the town. Plans for a new church were shelved but in 1882 the South Aisle was added, creating a doorway to the main street. Plans were rejected for a new site but others were put forward for a new church of cathedral proportions, primarily funded by the Bishop's own family on the existing sites. Funds became exhausted by 1910, but by then only the sanctuary, chancel and one bay of the nave were complete. These additions were then knitted to the existing building, although differences in level and direction necessitated the girder buttresses.

In spite of major campaigns to rebuild or complete the cathedral, its basic structure has remained much the same to this day. A famous Oban Cathedral Fund Appeal was run from New York in the United States by Mrs Alice Cisco, but it foundered with the Wall Street crash. Another was started by two Highland chiefs, Maclean of Duart and Cameron of Lochiel. Further work was undertaken in 1908 by Ian C Lindsay, by introducing the sliding glass doors and the raising of the floor level of the nave.

BONE

CATHEDRAL CHURCH OF CHRIST
OXFORD

In one of Britain's most attractive cities constructed in beautiful, mellow Cotswold stone college and cathedral sit side by side with the meadows and river close by. Although Christ Church is one of the smallest cathedrals in England, it administers the largest diocese, but far from imposing itself on the city, the building hides within the walls of the University. The college and cathedral occupy the site of the original priory of St Frideswide, the nun who became patron saint of Oxford and who died in 727. To this day there is an annual civic procession to her shrine. The present cathedral dates from around 1150.

In 1002 when the townspeople of Oxford realised that the invading Danes were taking refuge in the church, they set fire to it. This became known as the St Brice's day massacre.

In 1546 Henry VIII created the combination of college and cathedral from Cardinal's College, founded by Wolsey in 1525. The college and cathedral remain closely integrated; the college governors include the Dean and members of the cathedral chapter.

The choir, founded in 1525, sings each weekend during university term-time and the cathedral singers, a voluntary group drawn from the diocese as a whole, sings in many services.

The stone-built spire, although heavily restored, is one of the oldest in the country. Within the stone tracery of St Lucy's Chapel is a stained glass window depicting the murder of Thomas Becket. Under instruction from Henry VIII all of his images and pictures were to be destroyed. Though church authorities were very clever in the way they responded and by removing only the head of the archbishop the rest of the window was retained.

In 1523 Cardinal's College developed at great speed and expense, unfortunately four years later Cardinal Wolsey was disgraced and many of his projects were part finished. The magnificent coffin made originally for Wolsey was lost for years in Windsor, until rediscovered in 1806. It now contains the body of Lord Nelson in the crypt of St Paul's London.

Burne-Jones designed a window in the Latin Chapel depicting the life of St Frideswide. The window tells the legend of her pursuits by Algar, King of Leicester, who wanted to marry her. Her shrine, made in 1289, but destroyed and reconstructed in the 1880s.

From 1642 to 1646, Oxford was the loyalist headquarters and instead of its relaxed academic atmosphere the adjacent quadrangle buildings were busy with the comings and goings of generals and courtiers. King Charles I, a devout Anglican who attended the cathedral on a regular basis would receive them in the deanery garden and later in the Great Hall. The Cathedral Plate, together with that of many other colleges was sold to provide funds for the Royalist cause. After the Restoration new plate was purchased and this is now on exhibition in the Chapter House. The Tower to the Great Quadrangle was designed and built by Christopher Wren in 1682 and hosts the 6½ ton bell called Great Tom. At 9.05 every evening it tolls 101 times, the original number of students plus one by bequest.

No less than six British Prime Ministers were educated here in this unique combination of cathedral and college. Alice Liddel, better known as Alice in Wonderland, was born in Christ Church, daughter of the Dean whose long tenure lasted from 1855 to 1891, and it was here that The Reverend Charles Lutwidge Dodson (Lewis Carroll) set down in writing the unique stories which he had first told impromptu to his daughter. It was she who begged him to record these "fantastic adventures".

Some of the finest views of Oxford can be seen from Wren's other architectural masterpiece, the Cupola of the Sheldon Theatre.

ST NINNIAN CATHEDRAL PERTH

Consecrated in 1850, the cathedral stands on the site of the Blackfriars Monastery and is dedicated to St Ninian, the earliest name connected with Christianity in Scotland. The architect was William Butterfield, also responsible for Melbourne Cathedral and Keeble College.

The Lady Chapel and other additions to St Ninian's were the designs of Frank L Pearson. The Kinnoull Window, situated next to the cloister in the south aisle, incorporates portraits of the Kinnoull family as biblical figures with, for example, the Earl of Kinnoull shown as Lazarus. Near the window a brass plaque in Latin, is in memory of the children of Reverend J C Chambers who died in an outbreak of the plague.

The Founders Window in the north aisle shows St Serf reproaching St Mungo (St Kentigen) for leaving him at Culross, St Ninian holding a model of the cathedral and St Drostan with St Columba visiting Aberdour in Buchan, which was given to Columba by King Brude.

In the Chapel of St Andrew, completed in 1950 to celebrate the centenary of the cathedral, is a case displaying Bishop Torry's pastoral staff. This simple staff was used by a man in 1763 who travelled to rural areas holding services in barns

in secret, eventually becoming the first Bishop of the three united dioceses with a cathedral in Perth. Bishop Torry's tomb is on the north side of the altar.

The Bishop's Throne and Canon stalls are carved in oak, the two larger stalls for the Dean of the Diocese and the Provost of the Cathedral. The Bishop's Throne, nearest to the High Altar, displays embossed coats of arms of the three dioceses. The stalls have appropriate insignia on the canopies and the heraldic devices in the ceiling bosses include the city of Perth itself.

Situated in the former Resurrection Chapel at the west end of the cathedral is a simple wooden statue of Christ the King, a congregational memorial to R M Pullar. The wooden cross in this chapel is in memory of General Gordon and the window and brass plaque are a Black Watch memorial to those who fell in the South African War.

The baldacchino over the High Altar is carved in intricate detail in Cornish granite, and matches the stone used in the corresponding arcading. St George and St Andrew are featured on the pillars and the crucifixion on the central arch, while the altar incorporates a large slab of Iona marble.

For many years St Ninian's has been a training centre for clergy. They come to the cathedral for two years, live and work in Perth and many move on to become church rectors.

CATHEDRAL CHURCH OF ST PETER, ST PAUL AND ST ANDREW - PETERBOROUGH

The foundation of Christianity in this area dates from 665AD, through the influence of Peada, King of the Mercians. Situated on the edge of the Fens, Medeshamstede was the first name given to the settlement near the Benedictine Abbey and later renamed Burgh of St Peter. As with Ely Cathedral, Peterborough was gutted and sacked by the Danes in 870AD. It was reported by a Crowland Abbey monk that he buried 84 monks and many villagers. The Abbey was also attacked by Hereward the Saxon and a few years later the building was destroyed by fire.

Serious redesigning and construction began under Abbot John of Sais, the foundation stone laid in 1118. Abbot Benedict (1177) came from Canterbury, his effigy can be seen in the presbytery aisle. He continued to build in the Norman style whilst other cathedrals were concerned with developing the French Gothic, making Peterborough a co-ordinated style of the Romanesque. The magnificent wooden ceiling dates from 1220. This advanced and much increased Minster is much of the building we now see, taking some 80 years to complete and finally consecrated by Grosseteste, Bishop of Lincoln in 1237. Stone used in the construction was from the quarry of Barnack which was owned by the monastery.

In 1541 Henry VIII made the building a cathedral of a new diocese, permitting the retiring Abbot to continue as the first Bishop, a situation due in some part to the existence of the tomb of Catherine of Aragon, as the King had declared that it would contain one of the goodliest monuments in Christendom. Mary Queen of Scots was also buried here until her remains were removed to Westminster Abbey.

The building suffered serious neglect under the Stuarts and the commonwealth troops destroyed every fitting, monument and most of the furniture in the most destructive outbreak of iconoclasm in the country, rendering most material beyond repair. The Lady Chapel too was demolished by townsmen at a later date in order to sell the materials to raise money and carry out the essential structural repairs to the building.

On the fine west front are 3 13th century figures, Peter, Paul and Andrew to whom the cathedral is dedicated. There are also contemporary sculptures by Alan Durst.

Standing 3 metres high, a medieval windlass is positioned in the north west tower, used for hauling up stone, operated by walking on protruding pegs.

The brass lectern, the gift of Prior John Malden and Abbot William Ramsey (1471) is one of the few surviving medieval lecterns in the country.

CATHEDRAL CHURCH OF ST THOMAS OF CANTERBURY PORTSMOUTH

The Cathedral Church of St Thomas of Canterbury, in the dockside old town of Portsmouth, is one of the Anglican cathedrals which started life as a parish church.

It was a Norman merchant Jean de Gisors who, in the late 12th century, granted land for the monks of Southwick Priory to build a chapel 'to the glorious honour of the martyr Thomas of Canterbury, on my land which is called Sudewede, the island of Portsea'.

Badly damaged by gunners across the harbour in Gosport during the Civil War, the medieval building had been used by Royalists as a lookout post. Then, in the late 17th century, Charles II raised £9,000 to rebuild the nave and tower and as the borough and shipyard were enjoying a period of expansion and prosperity, transept galleries were added to hold the growing congregations.

When, in 1927, the new Diocese of Portsmouth was created, eminent architect Sir Charles Nicholson chose a scheme to echo the quire's classical late 17th century design, but all work stopped with the outbreak of the Second World War.

Today the visitor enters the completed cathedral at the western end through Michael Drury's vaulted walkway which acts as a covered gathering place on the way to worship. Now the link between the newly completed nave and the 17th century quire is the narrow dark space below the tower where the new font sits, made to a Greek design of the 9th century.

The medieval font, standing today near the nave's north door, was installed in 1508, the year the church re-opened after a closure lasting 60 years. Looking down is the 'Christus', Peter Ball's sculpture carved from oak driftwood and covered in part with gold leaf.

Among the works of art are Sir Charles Nicholson's ceramic plaque of the Virgin and Child by Florentine sculptor Andrea della Robbia, the painting 'The Miraculous Draught of Fishers' by celebrated local marine artist W L Wyllie, and the bronze statute of St John the Baptist by David Wynne, cast in 1951 to remember a Winchester College boy killed on the Matterhorn. In the Chapel of St Thomas is the Peace Globe made in 1985 by Highbury College students.

CATHEDRAL CHURCH OF ST PETER AND ST WILFRID
RIPON

In the 7th Century the Cathedral Church of St Peter and St Wilfrid was a monastery, founded in Ripon by Celtic monks from Iona and Melrose. St Wilfrid may well have been a native of the area and his enthusiasm for building expressed in his construction of the basilicas of Ripon and Hexham in the 10th century. The church was re-established as a foundation for secular canons and remained so during the Middle Ages, forming part of the very large diocese of York. It was promoted again to the rank of cathedral in 1836
.

The original building was extensively re-modelled by the first Norman Archbishop of York, Thomas of Bayeux in the latter end of the 11th century, but apart from the Norman Crypt, little remains of this period. The building was entirely reconstructed during the 12th century by Archbishop Roger of Pont L'Eveque, who was also concerned with the construction programme of York.

Ripon Cathedral stands on rising ground. The central western towers, originally designed with three lead spires, were lost during the Civil War and from a distance some impact has been lost. Scott removed tracery and mullions from the 1300s during the middle of the last century in an attempt to purify the appearance of the West Front.

The interior has six building periods in evidence, a patchwork of architectural styles reflecting the fashionable taste of archbishops through the centuries.

The Upper Chapel or Lady Loft was added about 1330 and is now used as a library. The bronze and marble pulpit erected in 1913 reflects the Arts and Crafts period, influenced by William Morris.

The expansion of the area focussed in Leeds, where the Industrial Revolution with factory produced textiles replaced the rural sheep farming in these parts. During the reformation the Archbishops of York suffered a reduction of status. A large church of this size was not appropriate to a town the size of Ripon, but by 1836 the local population had increased sufficiently to justify a separate diocese for this part of Yorkshire.

Ripon West Front, built around 1220, remains the strongest feature of the building, replacing the old and constantly copied Norman arcading with lancet windows, the early English style's new feature. Their deep setting combines with the strong corner turrets of the towers to create powerful shadowing.

CATHEDRAL CHURCH OF CHRIST AND THE BLESSED VIRGIN MARY - ROCHESTER

ochester has always been in a very strategic position, where the Roman road of Watling Street, between London and Dover, crosses the navigable estuary of the Medway.

With the exception of Canterbury, the Bishoprics of Rochester and London are the oldest in England, founded by St Augustine in 601. Justus was the first Bishop, sent from Rome by St Gregory to assist the Augustines' mission. Before the Conquest the area was subject to almost continuous war and the scarred Saxon building was finally demolished by Bishop Gundulf in 1080 and a new church begun by the Benedictine monks. Nothing of the original Saxon building remains but archaeologists have identified the foundations to the west of the existing nave.

William the Conqueror appointed Gundulf, the Norman monk, as Bishop from 1077-1108 because he had acquired a reputation for building, the Tower of London and Rochester Castle being examples of his work. Little of his original design remains. The Normans continued development of the building and a new cathedral was consecrated in 1130, an occasion attended by 13 Bishops and King Henry I. Later came the Gothic additions, the North Nave, Transept 1240-1255 being one of the finest examples.

The cathedral suffered severe damage when King John held it against the barons in the nearby Castle, and further desecration occurred when the soldiers of Simon de Montfort captured the city. The Reformation saw yet another period of iconoclasm and the building was further damaged during the last war.

The crypt is one of the finest in England with ribbed vaulting largely of 13th century construction. The crypt contains interesting, well-preserved tombs of bishops, in particular John de Sheppey, dating from 1360.

The first Rochester Cathedral was provided by Ethelbert, the first Christian king of England. Thomas Becket's martyrdom created great pilgrimages to Canterbury and economic advantages to the city but in 1201 William, a baker from Perth, was murdered in Rochester and the monks established his shrine as a pilgrimage centre.

The west door of Rochester Cathedral is the nearest comparable doorway to the great sculpted doorways of French Romanesque churches dating from around 1160. Illustrating 12 apostles on the lintel the tympanum has Christ in Majesty and although the quality of the work is still evident time has eroded much of it.

John Fisher and Nicholas Ridley were two Bishops at Rochester of particular note in the 16th century. Fisher, a friend of Erasmus and Thomas More, being Catholic and Ridley a Protestant. The deaths of both were centred on a move away from Catholicism by Henry VIII. Fisher fell from favour when, with Henry VIII, he refused to sanction the divorce of Catherine of Aragon. It was a refusal which brought his execution, as he became the first Bishop to be executed by the direction of a monarch.

Bishop Ridley, appointed in 1547, served the Protestant cause of Edward VI but found he could not accept the demands of his faith under Queen Mary. Consequently he was burnt at the stake at Oxford, accused of heresy after refusing to acknowledge the Roman doctrines. After the death of Mary in 1558 Protestantism returned under Elizabeth and Ridley's martyrdom was recognised.

In 1840 a fragment of a very fine Medieval painting was uncovered, named the Wheel of Fortune. This has been subsequently restored.

CATHEDRAL AND ABBEY CHURCH OF ST ALBAN
ST ALBANS

et back a little from the town of St Albans, the Cathedral's mellow brick tower is made of Roman tiles and bricks taken from the Roman town of Verulamium. A Benedictine church was founded by Offa in 793 and the Cathedral was begun by Abbott Paul of Caen.

Referred to by Bede, the eminent historian, Alban was a citizen of Verulamium. When refusing to accept the pagan gods the magistrates of the time condemned him to death and the church now stands on the site of his execution. St Alban, therefore, became the first Christian martyr of this country in 209AD.

During the reign of King Edgar in 960, attempts were made to rebuild the abbey church but Viking attacks put the project on hold. A large amount of building material had been assembled during this period and proved invaluable to the master mason Robert of Normandy, when re-building under the direction of Paul of Caen.

When the church was dedicated in 1115, it was the largest in England. A scriptorium was established which, in the 13th century would help Matthew Paris develop his skills. He illustrated the execution of St Alban and was also author of the first map of England.

In the same period, when a meeting took place here with King John and a group of disenchanted noblemen, the outcome was the sealing of Magna Carta in 1215.

After the collapse of two Norman pillars during a service in 1323, rebuilding began and

finished in 1345 under the Abbacy of Michael of Mentmore.

Born in 1100 at Abbots Langley, a village near St Albans, and with strong connections with the church here as his father was a monk at St Albans, Nicholas Breakspear became the only Englishman to be elected as Pope.

After the closure of the monastery Sir Richard Lee was appointed to destroy the monastic buildings and the materials to be sold for road repairs. The church survived and the townsfolk purchased this building for £400, but the upkeep proved a great burden on such a small market town and deterioration continued over 300 years.

When the Lady Chapel was used as a school, a Medieval bell originally used as a sanctus bell became the school bell after 300 years in regular use.

Lord Grimthorpe, designer of the mechanism of Big Ben, assumed control of raising funds for St Albans and in spite of disagreement with Sir George Gilbert Scott he continued to re-design and build with permission from the bishop, causing a great controversy which culminated in Parliament introducing the Ancient Monuments Protection Act.

Authors Note
All the paintings were begun in the 13th century, lime washed in the reign of Edward VII and partly uncovered in 1862. Since then further conservation and discovery has taken place. Professor Tristam was responsible for uncovering many of the Medieval wall paintings in the country. Later, Professor Baker, developed a system of removing the lime wash with a small pointed hammer and the two layers separated without a mark. Oyster shell palettes used for mixing colours by Medieval artists have been found in several churches.

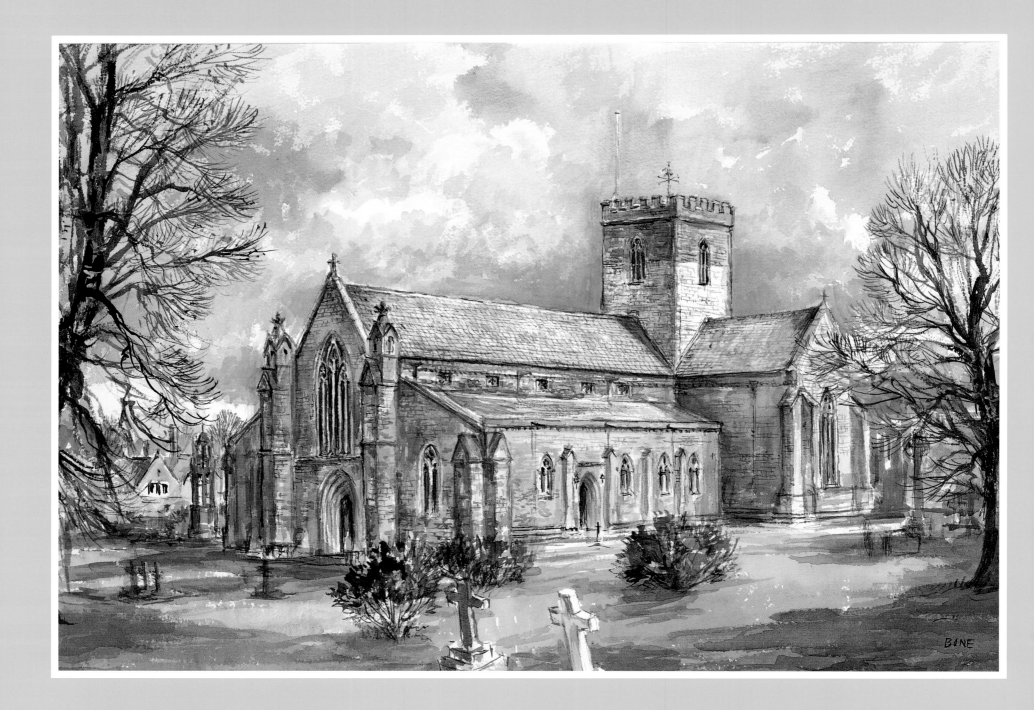

BONE

CATHEDRAL CHURCH OF ST KENTIGERN AND ST ASAPH
ST ASAPH

In the North East of Wales, St Asaph's Cathedral is the smallest ancient cathedral in Great Britain, founded by St Kentigern in 560AD. However, the building we now see was started in 1282 by Bishop Anian II. Extensive restoration took place by Scott in 1867 to 1875 and the interior has remained much as he left it. Amongst the valuable cathedral treasures is a copy of the 1588 translation of the Bible into Welsh.

There is no archaeological evidence of a church here before the 12th century. The life of St Kentigern written by Jocelyn in 1180 refers to the legend that a monastery and church was founded here between 560AD and 573AD. St Kentigern was Bishop of Strathclyde and founded a monastery at Llanelwy the Welsh name for St Asaph. Rhuddlan was in possession of the Normans from 1073 and they considered it expedient to protect their interests in the area and in 1143 the diocese of Llanelwy was formed.

Theobold Archbishop of Canterbury consecrated Gilbert the first bishop. The site of the cathedral was in the path of war between English Kings and Welsh Princes. How much destruction occurred during this time is not known. Bishop Anian II, whose effigy is in the south aisle, sought the protection of King Edward I and in so doing withstood the enmity of Llywelyn ap Gruffydd.

In 1282 there was an accidental burning of the cathedral by the English military. Anian excommunicated the soldiers and by so doing fell out of favour with Edward I, never more to enjoy his confidence.

In 1402 Owain Glyndwr and his troops destroyed all the fittings, books and altars together with three manors. Bishop John Trefor II was a sympathiser of his cause and was quickly replaced by Robert de Lancaster, who directed the repairs and re-roofing. Destruction

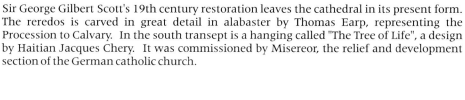

again occurred in the Commonwealth period and Bishop John Owen, chaplain to Charles I, was imprisoned in the tower.

Military building work at Caernarfon has influenced the rebuilding of the cathedral from time to time. In all probability some work was undertaken by Master Walter of Hereford and Master Henry of Ellerton.

Purple sandstone found in parts of the building of the cathedral was quarried two miles away. The building was part financed by rectorial tithes administered by Bishop Llywelyn in the late 13th century and pilgrims were encouraged to give alms to the church as they visited the shrine of St Asaph.

The bishops throne was designed by Scott and is a memorial to Bishop William Beveridge. The canons stalls were made by William Frankelyn, master carpenter of Chester and Flint, dating from 1418, the time of Bishop Redman. They remain the sole surviving examples of canopied stalls in North Wales.

The pulpit is a memorial to Bishop Thomas Vowlershort, a great educationalist who inspired the forming of church schools and the restoration of churches to which he gave generously.

Sir George Gilbert Scott's 19th century restoration leaves the cathedral in its present form. The reredos is carved in great detail in alabaster by Thomas Earp, representing the Procession to Calvary. In the south transept is a hanging called "The Tree of Life", a design by Haitian Jacques Chery. It was commissioned by Misereor, the relief and development section of the German catholic church.

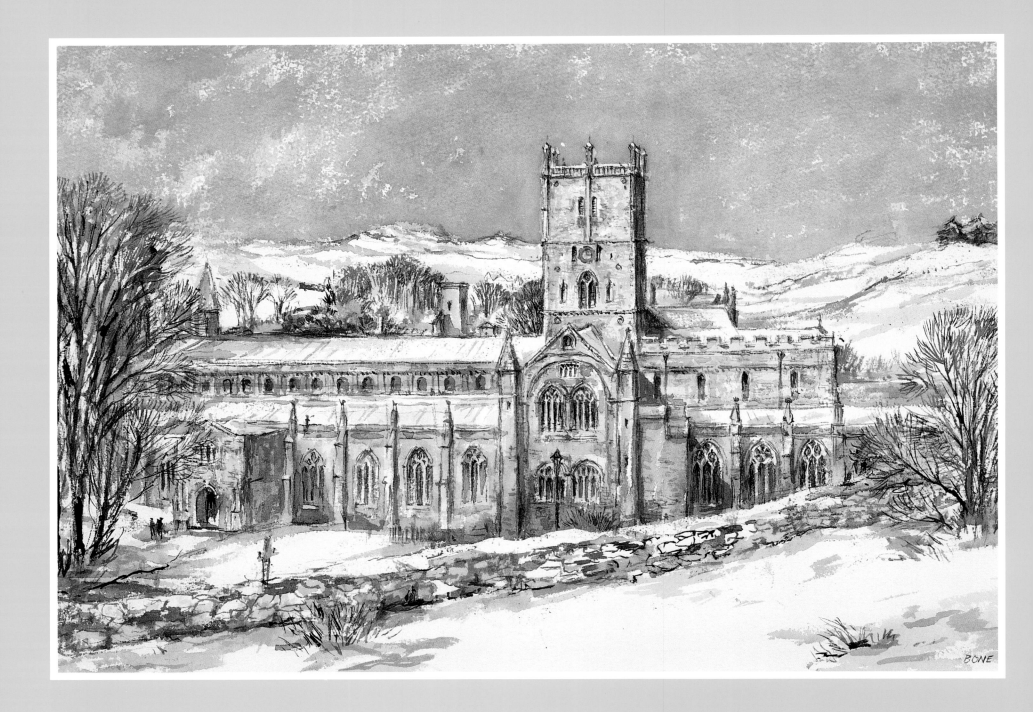

CATHEDRAL CHURCH OF ST ANDREW AND ST DAVID
ST DAVIDS

t David and his monks built the first church on this site which was destroyed by fire in 645. The Danes invaded and killed Bishop Abraham and sacked the building in 1078. In 1115 the first Norman bishop was enthroned, converting the Celtic monastic way to a diocesan organisation.

Peter de Leia, a Florentine monk, previously Prior of Wenlock Abbey became the third Norman Bishop and the first of the great builders. St David's was at this time in a ruined state and he began rebuilding in 1180, using Cambrian sandstone, quarried from Caerfai and Caerbwdy.

The tower fell in 1220 and an earthquake in 1248 did even more damage. Bishop Gower, 1328, added the south porch and founded a chantry in the Lady Chapel. Bishop Martins tomb is also attributed to him.

Late in the 15th Century the roofs of the building were completely renovated and the tower was increased to its present height under the supervision of Bishop Vaughan. However, during the Civil War lead was stripped from the roofs, Lady Chapel and aisles, leaving this area exposed to the weather. The Medieval library was also destroyed. But later Chapter Orders show that the Canons reduced their income in order to raise the £1,500 necessary to effect the repairs.

The nave with the roof of Irish oak is attributed to Owen Pole 1472-1509. The square pendants feature the Welsh dragon and traces of painting are still visible on some of the

piers. Below the tower the Choir has 28 stalls dating from Bishop Tully's episcopate in the 15th Century. The first prebendal stall is marked by the Royal arms for the reigning sovereign, a unique feature peculiar to St David's. The Bishops Throne was reconstructed by Scott.

Encaustic tiles, dating from the 15th Century, have designs of the Beauchamp and Berkeley Arms and can be seen on some areas of flooring. These are in the rich earth colours of the Malvern clay. Some are broken, reputed to be the result of Cromwell's army when they rode up to the altar on horseback and began desecrating the building.

The central tower was in a precarious state when Sir George Gilbert Scott began restoration in 1863. Cavities in the masonry were filled with liquid cement and, for the first time, the foundations were drained and in the course of this work relics, thought to be that of St David and St Justinian, were discovered.

Before the high altar stands the tomb of Edmund Tudor father of Henry VII. Originally in Greyfriars Church, Carmarthen, it was moved by order of Henry VIII and the disollution of the monasteries. On the north side of the Presbytery are the remains of St David's shrine. Originally relics were placed in a reliquary and an ancient order states that in case of battle these should be taken a day's journey from the city.

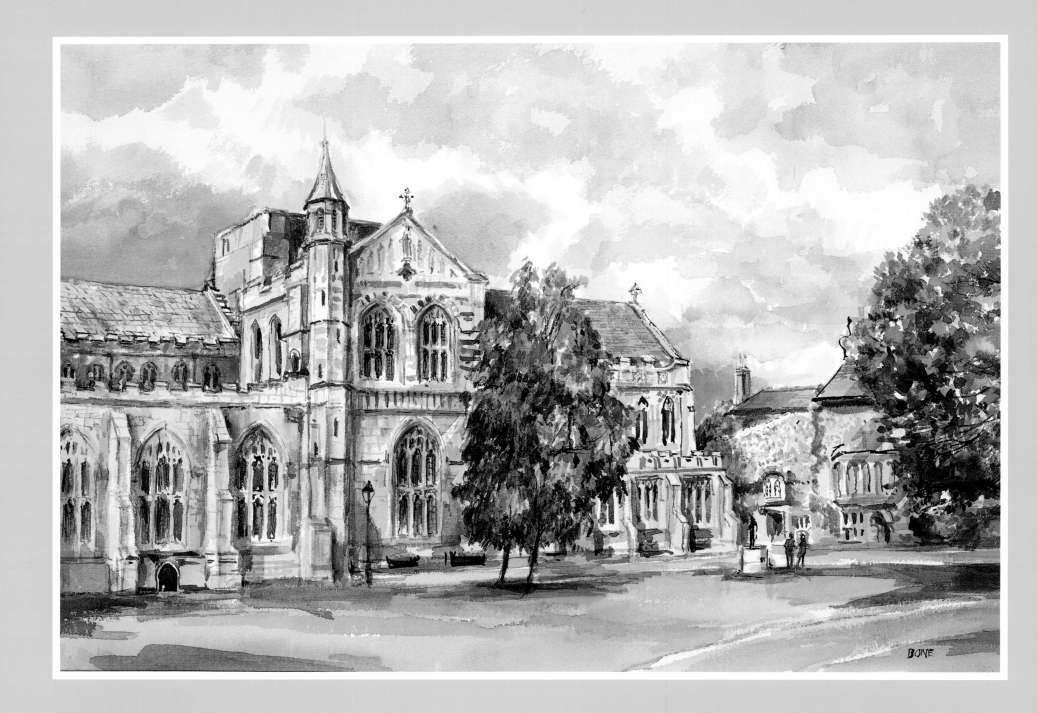

CATHEDRAL CHURCH OF ST JAMES
ST EDMUNDSBURY AND IPSWICH

 igeberght, King of the East Angles, hoped to retire to a monastery in what is now presumed Bedericesworth, the old name for Bury St Edmunds. The abbey of Bury, a great centre for medieval pilgrimages, was dedicated to the martyrdom of St Edmund, another 9th century king of East Angles.

When the Danes' tax increases hit this part of Suffolk, the body of St Edmund was removed to London in 1010 but thanks to Bury St Edmunds' benefactor Cnut, a church was built to house the Saint's remains, and the shrine entrusted to Benedictine monks.

Edward the Confessor granted the abbey the right to mint money and abbotts held court with legal power in Suffolk. Attempts were made by Arfast, Bishop of East Anglia, to establish a cathedral at Bury St Edmunds but in about 1096 Norwich became the seat of the East Anglian diocese. Henry VIII pursued the idea of a separate See but the diocese of Bury St Edmunds and Ipswich was only finally achieved in 1914.

William of Worcester visited the church in 1479 suggesting the original Norman church may well have been 200 feet long, but little evidence remains. In 1503 rebuilding commenced on the nave and finished in the reign of Edward VI, who partly financed the building.

The master mason responsible for this spectacular Perpendicular nave was John Wastell, who lived in Crown Street. He also designed the fan vaulting in Peterborough Cathedral.

New work extended the western bay to the street line, the earlier church being contained within the abbey precinct. Fragments of 16th century glass were incorporated in a window dating from 1850 on the south side, including the theme of a Jesse tree, probably made in Rouen.

Surrounding the walls of the Choir, are the coats of arms of the groups of Barons sworn to enforce the terms of the Magna Carta. This was the result of a meeting held at the abbey to put pressure on King John to grant a charter of liberties. Originally the Norman tower was built as a bell tower and entrance gate for St James' Church and was not separated as it is today. The present Abbey gate replaces one destroyed by riots in 1327 and completed in 1384, which was built mainly for defensive purposes although an excellent example of decorated design.

The crossing and choir were consecrated in 1970 but the chancel designed by Scott was too small for large cathedral services and orchestral events, and a new development was commissioned, designed by Steven Dykes Bower, cathedral architect from 1943 to 1988.

Dykes Bower had left a bequest to continue works on the cathedral unfinished in 1970. The bequest, however, was not sufficient to complete the building of the new tower and a new design, based on Dykes Bower's drawings, was amended by Hugh Mathew B.ARCH.ARIBA. This plan was awarded a grant by the Millennium Commission in 1997 and they are co-funding the project with the Cathedral Council.

CATHEDRAL CHURCH OF THE BLESSED VIRGIN MARY
SALISBURY

The See was first founded in 1075 at the ancient roman fortress of Old Sarum, on an imposing hill two kilometres from the present city. By the 13th century the church was too small and inconvenient and so it was decided to build a completely new cathedral on a new site and work began under Bishop Poore, who gained a sanction from the Pope in 1220. Works continued under the direction of Bishops Bingham, William of York and Giles of Bridport and in 1258 the building was consecrated in the presence of Henry III.

The stone used for the foundations came from Purbeck in Dorset and the master mason responsible was Nicholas of Ely. The cathedral close, the finest in England, was based on a plan allowing for the building of private residences for the canons. The unparalleled views of the cathedral were appreciated in full by John Constable and William Turner in many sketches and in the finished works of Salisbury.

The building was completed in a relatively short time and, therefore, more co-ordinated in the design of early English Gothic. With 6,500 tons of stonework forming the tower and spire, buttresses and braces were necessary. The octagonal spire is the tallest in Britain. In 1091 a school was formed by Bishop Osmund for the boys of the choir. Over the centuries this developed into the Salisbury Cathedral School, housed in the former Bishop's Palace, continuing the rich choral tradition established originally in the cathedral in Old Sarum. More recently a separate girl's choir was formed in 1991, sharing the tours, recordings and daily services in the cathedral with the boy's choir.

Above the delightful misericords of the stalls are arms of the earlier bishops of Salisbury. There are two notable brasses. One commemorates Bishop Gheast who bequeathed a large library to the cathedral. The other is to Bishop Wyville reflecting his mid 14th century achievement in returning Sherbourne Castle to the ownership of the cathedral from the Earl of Salisbury.

One of the four surviving original copies of the Magna Carta is on display in the Chapter House. Written in Latin, the document has been in the cathedral archives for some 800 years.

The footpath to Harnham Mill signals the rural setting south of the cathedral, where Anthony Trollope formed his observations on the families of clergy for his Barchester novels. Thomas Hardy's Melchester is, of course, based on Salisbury.

Amongst the many 20th century artistic contributions to the cathedral is the bronze by Dame Elisabeth Frink of the Walking Madonna, positioned in the Cathedral Close, and the glass engraving by Laurence Whistler to commemorate his brother Rex Whistler the mural painter killed in Normandy in 1944.

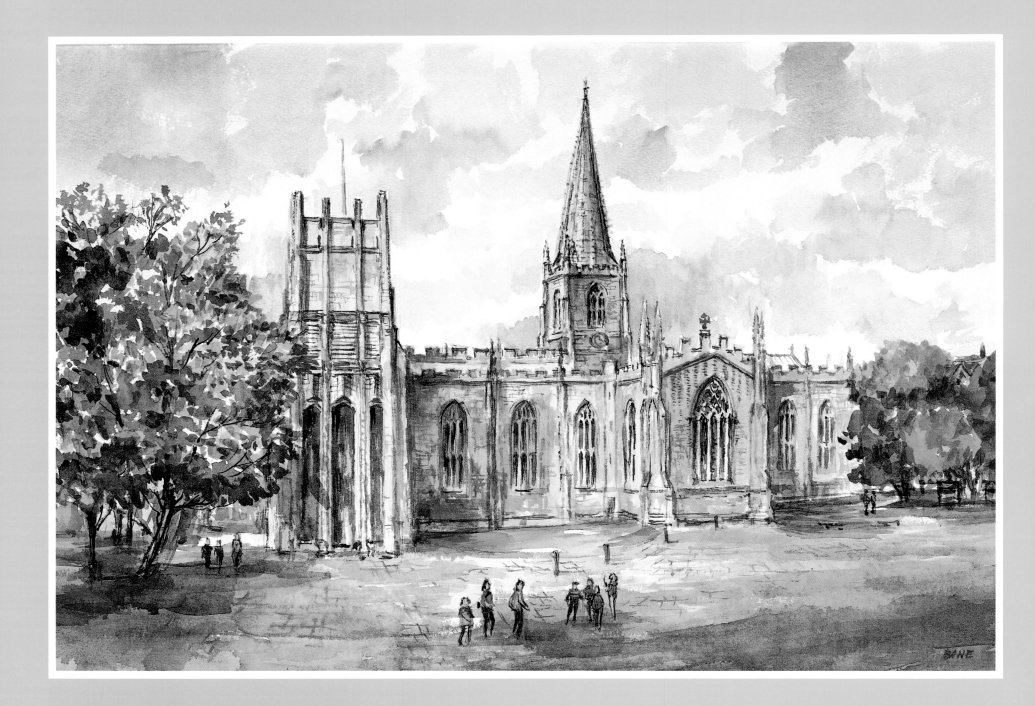

CATHEDRAL CHURCH OF ST PETER AND ST PAUL SHEFFIELD

William the Conqueror devastated this part of Yorkshire. The Domesday Book mentions no church in Sheffield but the fragment of an old Mercian cross, now in the British Museum, traces the site as a centre of worship since the 9th century.

About 1100 William de Lovelot, Lord of the Manor of Hallam, built a church here and some evidence of the early stonework can be seen in the wall of the east Sanctuary. A later church followed, dedicated by Wickwan Archbishop of York but this was later demolished or devastated in the Barons' War.
Sheffield church was impoverished by the passing of the Chantries Act in 1547 but some courageous people petitioned Queen Mary in 1553 to restore sufficient property to the church to guarantee a continuing ministry. This request was granted to 12 capital burgesses, their office still exists and meetings are still held in the cathedral.

When the monasteries were threatened with dissolution the fourth Earl of Shrewsbury decided on Sheffield as a safer family burial place. His very fine tomb shows him dressed in armour, wearing a coronet and the Mantle of the Garter. The oak screen on the far side of the cathedral introduces St Katherine's Chapel, the church was extended here in 1520 to accommodate a private chantry for the

Earls of Shrewsbury.

John Wesley preached in Paradise Square in Sheffield, at which time he was still an Anglican priest. It is believed that he preached in Sheffield church and that Wesley's preaching desk is now in the cathedral sacristy.

The mensa of the altar is pre-Reformation, discovered in 1864. It is in two parts previously used face down as paving stones. The reredos recognises the seven chapels in the ancient church and is carved in alabaster.
Christopher Webb designed the very fine tedeum window Christ in glory flanked by prophets Paul, Barnabas and John the Baptist, all surmounted by the dove of peace. The Chapel of St George carries the remembrance of those who served their country and the colours of the Coldstream Guards and the Jack and Ensign of HMS Sheffield.

The industrial revolution has had a profound effect upon Sheffield, which has developed from a small country to economy to one of England's largest and most enterprising cities.

The present perpendicular church was built about 1430.

CATHEDRAL CHURCH OF ST GERMAN
SODOR AND MAN

The diocese of Sodor and Man consists today solely of the Isle of Man but earlier it included several of the Western Islands of Scotland. When St Patrick's Island was in the possession of Norse Kings, the first cathedral was founded by Simon of Argyl, a former Abbott of Iona and he became Bishop in 1226.

Anglo-Scottish conflict meant that the Isle of Man changed hands several times. After 1333 the Lords of Man refortified St Patrick's Island and the cathedral was completed. However, by the 17th century this building became dilapidated, the chancel was partly used as a Parish Church and is now a ruin preserved by the Manx National Heritage.

In 1870 Bishop Hill found the task of raising money for restoration impossible, in spite of being very successful in raising money in his previous years at Sheffield. Although his great wish was to restore the old building there was no support for this, financial or otherwise. After considerable debate as to whether the cathedral be in Peel or Douglas the project was abandoned but the large Chapel of St Nicholas at Bishop's Court, Kirkmichael where the Bishop has his home became the pro-cathedral.

A large Parish Church was still required by Peel. Bishop Hill raised money by preaching on

the island and in England and his offer of £6,000 from these proceeds for a new church was accepted in 1879, the site selected by Hill was purchased for £505 and the foundation stone, made by Archdeacon Moore, was laid on the 21 August 1879 in the presence of Governor Loch and the Bishop.

An architect from Liverpool was responsible for the design and the project completed by 1884. It had been hoped that the new church would be consecrated as a cathedral in time for Queen Victoria's Golden Jubilee celebrations but the sudden death of Bishop Hill and further disputes between Douglas and Peel created further delays and Bishop's Court provided a temporary solution. The new church was finally consecrated as a cathedral in 1980.

The Isle of Man is full of legend, one legend relates to St Patrick, who may have sailed his curragh to land on a tiny island off what is now Port of Peel in 444AD on his way to Ireland, spending some time converting the native people to Christianity. The greater part of the Isle is closed within the walls of Peel Castle. St Patrick's Church is now a small ruined keeil.

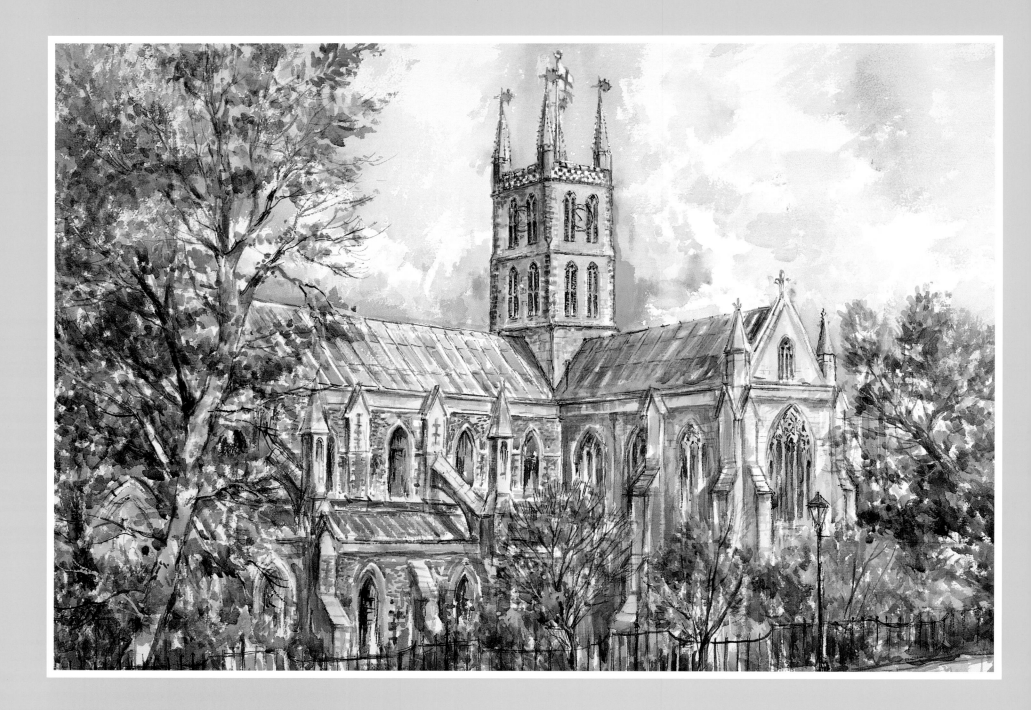

CATHEDRAL AND COLLEGIATE CHURCH OF ST SAVIOUR AND ST MARY OVERIE - SOUTHWARK

The Cathedral Church of St Saviour, the College of Priests, was established by St Swithun on this site, though the establishment changed with the installation of the Augustinian Canons in 1106 who continued to serve the church until the Reformation. A few Norman features remain but the building developed to its present form during the 13th century by Bishop Peter des Roches of Winchester, who reshaped the nave, quire and later retroquire in the early English style.

Today, the long history of Southwark comes into focus with parts of the Roman Villa still visible. The first proof of a church existing on the site occurs in the Domesday Book of 1086 with records of a monasterium during the reign of Edward the Confessor. It had its own profitable wharf for handling goods brought up the River Thames.

Two knights, William Pont de l' Arche and William Dauncey founded the new church of St Mary Overie. Part of the duties of the canons of St Augustine then serving the church included the care of the sick. With that purpose they built a hospital dedicated to St Thomas of Canterbury, relocated now to St Thomas's Hospital in Lambeth. Yet another fire followed in the 15th Century, the rebuilding undertaken by Cardinal Beaufort at his own expense.

After the Reformation the building was allowed to deteriorate until work began in the middle of the 19th century. The reconstruction of the nave was so appalling that A W Pugin forced its demolition. The present version was built by Sir Arthur Blomfield in 1897. The church was raised to Collegiate status and became a Cathedral in 1905.

Before its role as a cathedral it was known as the Actors' Parish Church, being near to the Globe Theatre at Bankside. The parish register is full of names listed in the first folio edition of Shakespeare, when baptisms, weddings and funerals were frequented by the players of the time. There are eight monuments in the cathedral connected with literature and players. The monument to William Shakespeare in the south aisle, commemorates the most famous parishioner of Southwark. The design shows the playwright lying in a Southwark field with the church, the Globe and Winchester Palace carved in relief behind. The stained glass memorial window to Shakespeare is designed by Christopher Webb and shows Prospero, Ariel and Caliban and other characters from his comedies and tragedies.

To bring things nearer to our own time another tablet is dedicated to Sam Wanamaker who was largely responsible for the inspiration to re-build the Globe Theatre at Bankside.

Southwark Cathedral is an architectural gem and difficult to find through a mass of tiny streets, adjacent to one of London's oldest markets. With building land at such a high premium the cathedral is surrounded by towering buildings but a plan now exists to clear a vista to view the cathedral from the Thames Embankment.

CATHEDRAL AND PARISH CHURCH OF
THE BLESSED VIRGIN MARY - SOUTHWELL

Southwell is the smallest cathedral town in England, the cathedral's two spires rising from the Nottinghamshire landscape. For centuries Southwell's Cathedral Church of the Blessed Virgin Mary formed a supplementary Bishop's Stool of the York diocese. The first church on the site was built by Paulinus, the missionary Bishop of York in the 7th century. The Saxon church was demolished, supervised by Archbishop Thomas of Bayeux and apart from the eastern section most of the remaining structure dates from this period. The conical spires on the west front were reconstructed in the last century. Magnificent carving in stone of the Capitals and arches, are a great feature of the cathedral. Foliage, birds and animals are the finest to be found of their period but the master carver is unknown.

The Manor of Southwell was given by King Eadwig to Oskydel, Archbishop of York, in 956AD, and a college was established a century later. As a collegiate church the Minster, a Saxon word for a large church which administers an area, served as a sub-cathedral much as Ripon did in the West Riding of Yorkshire. The collegiate status survived the Reformation period and Southwell became the cathedral of the new diocese of Southwell in 1884.

The west front of the cathedral is considered to be the finest Norman example in England and dates from 1140, though the window is a 15th century insertion. The door on this elevation is 12th century with contemporary iron fittings. In the nave is a font from the 17th century. At Southwell there was a school of restoration and font carvers and examples of their craft can be seen in some of the local churches in the area. Towards the Sanctuary

Flemish glass illuminates the east end of the nave, originally coming from Temple Church in Paris and was presented to Southwell by Henry Gally Knight, Member of Parliament and poet. The carved leaves of Southwell are of international reputation.

The Chapter House was built at the end of the 13th century at the transitional time when early English was moving towards the Decorated style. The Chapter House is the only octagonal Chapter House in England with a vaulted stone roof unsupported by a central pillar.

The doorway has one delicate central column and marble shafts in the side columns, but it is the carving that is so intricate throughout. Bramble, pine, oak and vine are all carved and completed with such artistry. The sculptor or group of carvers is unknown. The carving continues over the canopied recesses made for the canons' seats. Fragments of medieval glass are set in the windows amongst the clear glass of the tracery windows.

At the east end of the north aisle is the Airmens' Chapel. The altar was made in the workshops of RAF Norton as a memorial to those from Norton who lost their lives in the Great War. It was presented to the Minster in 1919 and made from parts of aircraft destroyed in the air battles over France.

The Kelham Madonna by Alan Coleman is amongst the 20th century sculptures and the work shows the influence of Frank Dobson RA, his one-time professor. The tryptic by Hamish Moyle of the Little Gidding community is inspired by a poem by Dame Edith Sitwell. "Still falls the rain …".

CATHEDRAL CHURCH OF ST MARY
TRURO

I t was the Celtic missionary saints who established the foundations of the church in Cornwall, which from 1050 came under the diocese of Exeter. It was only 800 years later that Truro was established as a separate diocese, when Edward White Benson, formerly Chancellor of Lincoln Cathedral and headmaster of Wellington College, was appointed Bishop.

John Loughborough Pearson RA was appointed architect for the first Anglican cathedral to be built since St Paul's. Part of the old parish church of St Mary is still evident in the design, particularly the Perpendicular remains. In spite of the collapse of the Cornish economy with the closure of mines, funds were available and the then Prince of Wales laid the foundation stones. Pearson's expertise in vaulting and the strong influence of the Gothic skills of Scott meant that the Cornish people were given a brilliant example of the perfect Gothic cathedral.

Although consecrated in 1259 the parish church was rebuilt about 1550. Pearson succeeded in retaining the aisle in spite of opposition from the Bishop who would have had it demolished. The typical barrel roof is enriched by coloured, carved bosses by John Harvey, a priest, and designed by John Philips.

The site itself was very restricted and Pearson had to accommodate his grand design within a length of only 300ft. Though the nave is only 65 feet wide and there is only 70 feet to the crown of the vault, the effect is surprisingly spacious.

Within the Chapel of Unity and Peace are memorials to three leading Cornish statesmen. Sir John Eliot, the Lord High Treasurer, Sidney Earl of Godolphin and Sir William Molesworth, Secretary for the Colonies.

In the North Transept is a large Elizabethan alabaster monument to the Robartes family which was probably carved in Nottingham and assembled by local craftsmen here, a product of a period in English sculpture much under-estimated. There is also is a painting of Cornubia, land of the saints, featured as part of the centenary celebrations in 1980 and unveiled by HRH The Prince of Wales as Duke of Cornwall.

A unique stone sculpture of St Nicholas, originally from Brittany, stands at the entrance to St Mary's Aisle. The carving, about six centuries old, shows a group of children carved into a tub at the feet of the saint (Santa Claus).

The figures on the reredos behind the small altar in the South Transept represent four missionaries, St Paul, St Boniface, St Sampson and Truro born Henry Martyn, (1781-1812), a missionary who served in Turkey, Persia and India. The Breton pieta, carved in the 14th century is a beautiful semi-naive sculpture of the crucified Jesus in the arms of Mary, the patron saint of this cathedral.

John Wesley, who had a profound influence on Christianity in Cornwall, is portrayed preaching in the Gwennap Pit in one of the lancet windows made by Clayton and Bell.

CATHEDRAL CHURCH OF ALL SAINTS
WAKEFIELD

In the 10th century the original Saxon church stood on a crossroads on the land between the Calder and Aire rivers. Some evidence of this period is still provided by the shaft of the Saxon preaching cross which was originally positioned near the town well, while excavations in 1974 revealed a Saxon church which was a small structure within the present site.

Wakefield had been a Royal Manor since the Saxons and considered to be in an important strategic position at the crossing of the rivers and, in 1090, William Rufus gave the Manor to the second Earl of Warenne. At this time the population was about 30 families. Eventually the churches of Wakefield and Sandal Magna came under the control of the Priory of Lewes and they continued to draw income from this source but the building remained the responsibility of the local people.

About 1100 the first Norman church came into being. During the 12th century, at the time of the Crusades, Wakefield was playing a pivotal role in the growth of the wool trade and the church was expanded. Further expansion occurred

during the time of Henry II and Richard Coeur de Leon and the people of Wakefield expanded their church again in the 13th century over the existing churchyard.

The Early English pillars illustrate a change in building design, but about 1300 the tower collapsed across the building towards the North West, destroying much of the building. Wealthy merchants would rebuild the church doubling the height, and during the rebuilding programme the congregation used St John's Chapel, Northgate.

With the church without a tower, money was rather used for financing the beginning of the Hundred Years' War and, when the river bridge collapsed, further funds had to be diverted.

In spite of the Wars of the Roses, the citizens of Wakefield continued to improve the church during the 15th century and the tower was completed in 1420. By the 19th century the patchwork of repairs of the previous 150 years brought pressure for a major rebuild. First the tower and spire were renewed, then the galleries removed and by 1874 the interior looked very much as it does today.

CATHEDRAL CHURCH OF THE HOLY TRINITY
AND ST PETER - WINCHESTER

Two centuries after the Romans left Winchester the King of the West Saxons was baptised, converted by Birinus who was sent by Pope Honorius. A minster or large church was built by Cenwalh, son of Cynegils in 670. Bishop Haeddi transferred the cathedra from Dorchester on Thames to Winchester, making the city the most prominent in Wessex.

The foundations of Cenwalh's original church were excavated in 1960 and marked with a brick outline north of the present cathedral. Winchester was the ancient capital of Wessex and several Wessex kings and kings of all England are buried here, Alfred the Great being the most significant.

A new minster was founded by Alfred's son Edward in 903. With the further development of Nunnaminster, a convent, the Bishop's Palace of Wolvesey and the Royal Palace this became the largest religious complex in the country, occupying a quarter of the walled city.

Archbishop Dunstan and King Edgar supported Bishop Ethelwold in introducing the Benedictine order in place of secular canons and St Swithin's Priory continued for the next 600 years.

The minster became the largest Anglo-Saxon church in England. Following the Norman Conquest Bishop Walkelin was appointed to develop an even larger church following the Romanesque style. The foundations were laid in 1079 and the site was within the existing boundaries so that the new building could develop alongside the old minster.

Pilgrims would visit the shrine of St Swithun in great numbers. Over the centuries the relics were moved until finally in 1538 they were destroyed by officers of the Henry VIII Commission for the Destruction of Shrines. Most of the 11th century church has been rebuilt but the crypt still survives though subject to flooding.

Earlier this century William Walker, the deep sea diver, worked six hours a day for five years underpinning the foundations with concrete. When the marshy foundations had caused the central tower to collapse in 1107 it was blamed on King William Rufus who was buried beneath it, his evil influence supposedly causing disaster.

Bishop William Wykeham, Chancellor of England, statesman and founder of Winchester College and New College Oxford, was one of the great influences of the cathedral.

In the mid 17th century parliamentary troops rode horses through the cathedral, destroying the altar and burning the communion rail and prayer books. Priceless books in the library have survived, including the 12th century Winchester Bible, Bishop George Morley expanded the collection by bequeathing 2,000 books.

Two famous writers of books are interred. In the north nave of the aisle is the grave of Jane Austen and in the Silkstede Chapel that of Izaak Walton.

CATHEDRAL CHURCH OF CHRIST AND THE BLESSED VIRGIN MARY - WORCESTER

Worcester Cathedral enjoys a wonderful position, raised on the banks of the River Severn, and watched over by the many Royal swans and by supporters at the county cricket ground watching their team perform against this stunning backdrop.

For 600 years, from the end of the first Millennium, the cathedral was the centre of a flourishing community of monks who followed the Rule of St Benedict. As well as their religious and classical learning, the monks ran a hospital for the thousands of pilgrims visiting the precincts.

St Oswald was Worcester's great 10th century saint, whose church was destroyed in 1041 by the raiding Danes. Its second bishop, Wulfstan, was the only member of the Saxon hierarchy who approved of the Norman reforms, managing to retain his office after the invasion and adding his own Norman church in 1084. Parts of his work have survived, notably the Crypt.

When Wulfstan was canonised in 1203 his shrine became a popular place of pilgrimage, but just 13 years later, King John's burial in the cathedral meant more pilgrims and increased revenue. The codicil to his will in which the King ordered that he be buried in the cathedral is preserved to this day in the library.

William Shockerwick, Master Mason of Worcester from 1316-1324, honed his skills in the Somerset quarries. His vigorously carved misericords date from 1379 and feature the day-to-day occupations of the monks. The chapter house was often a small room, a chapter being read before the transactions of the day, but the importance of the cathedral demanded a separate building so in 1115 a circular Chapter House was built with a central pillar to support the vault.

Bishop William de Blois developed the Lady Chapel in the Early English style. Progressively the early Romanesque church of Wulfstan was demolished and replaced by a Gothic style of architecture, though development was curtailed when the Black Death decimated the local population.

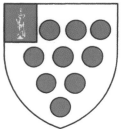

Amongst the great events held here was the funeral of Prince Arthur in 1502. He died at Ludlow Castle aged 15, soon after marrying Catherine of Aragon. Arthur was the eldest son of Henry VII and heir to the throne. His younger brother became Henry VIII and also married Catherine.

Worcester has the earliest of the perpendicular cathedral towers, completed in 1374, with a timber lead covered spire, later demolished. The Reformation saw the destruction of the shrines of Oswald and Wulfstan and in 1540 the existing monastery was dissolved. During the Civil War the Royalists were commanded by the Duke of Hamilton, who died of his wounds in a house known as the Commandery - near the cathedral. He is buried before the high altar in the cathedral. The Royalists lost the famous Battle of Worcester and King Charles II fled the area. Bishop Horne, a puritan, pulled down the Chapter House and part of the cloisters, while Cromwell's men removed Dallamn's organ which vanished along with the cathedral glass.

Later developments during the Victorian period secured the fabric of the building, although some architectural features may not be to the taste of all. Many windows were replaced, among them the west window, an outstanding example of Victorian glass, telling the story of the Creation. There is also a fine collection of Victorian sculpture.

Sir Edward Elgar was born a few miles away and his music features in the many concerts given in the cathedral. A plaque in the cathedral celebrates his career as Master of the King's Music and the Elgar window depicts "The Dream of Gerontius".

Worcester has a very distinguished choral tradition, with a repertoire which includes English and continental music and Worcester takes turns with Gloucester and Hereford at hosting the Three Choirs Festival.

CATHEDRAL CHURCH OF ST PETER
YORK

ork was the principal settlement of the Brigantes Tribe. Altira Romana, as it was known, became the base for Roman Emperors during their visits to England. Constantine was proclaimed Emperor in 306 in the Basilica that once stood under the present South Transept. In 312 Constantine issued an edict of toleration for Christianity.

King Edwin was baptised by Bishop Paulinus in 627 and York was, for a time, the capital city of England. In 601 with Papal authority Saint Augustin appointed 12 Bishops and it was agreed that power to ordain further Bishops be awarded to York and Canterbury.

After many years of sporadic visits to the coastal areas, the Viking Army wintered in England in 855. Then the Danes captured York and after a period of eight years, during which the See of York was vacant, West Saxon armies and Norse raiders became alternate occupiers of the city. It was not until Edgar became King that the English took firm control.

Following the Norman Conquest, Aedred a Saxon Bishop, officiated at the Coronation of William at Westminster Abbey, much to the concern of his fellow countrymen. An uprising occurred in 1068 and the City was burnt. Thomas of Bayeux was appointed to the See in 1070, and rebuilding of the cathedral began ten years later.

The Crypt was constructed under the direction of Bishop Roger of Pont L' Evéque between 1154 and 1181, but the building did not match the importance of the See and so rebuilding of the present Transepts began, between 1227 and 1260. The central tower was not completed until the early 15th century.

York, the largest medieval cathedral in the country with a great collection of medieval glass, was also a great centre for religion and education and the Great Library was unparalleled north of the Alps. Such was its reputation that the scholar Alcuin was called by Charlemagne to revive education standards throughout Europe.

The construction of the Minster as we know it now began in 1220 when Archbishop Gray decided to create a cathedral as a rival to Canterbury. The South Transept was built in the early English Gothic manner, and the sub-dean John Romanus is credited with the building of the great central tower, originally topped by a wooden spire which collapsed in 1407. The reconstruction continued uninterrupted for 250 years.

The Chapter House, begun in 1260, was where members of the Chapter administered what amounted to the richest corporation in the North. The Dean, as Chairman, retained the right enthrone a new Archbishop, and while the Chancellor oversaw the educational standards of the grammar school and the preaching and theological abilities of clergy.

In 1349 reconstruction was delayed when the master mason and many craftsmen working on the cathedral fell victim to the Black Death. In 1405 Bishop Skirlaw commissioned the glazing of the east window of the Lady Chapel by John Thornton of Coventry, a fine example of medieval glass.

The middle of the 15th century saw the growing influence of the conflict between the houses of Lancaster and York. Archbishop George Neville, brother of the Earl of Warwick, was enthroned at York Minster, at the celebrations that followed the Neville family underlined their Yorkist allegiance. Chief guest was the Duke of Gloucester, later Richard III.

In the Chapter House on the 5 May 1535 Archbishop Lee declared that the Bishop of Rome had no greater jurisdiction in the realm than any other foreign dignitary. During a later visit to York by Henry VIII, Dean Richard Layton destroyed the Saint William's Shrine as a protest against Popery. During the reign of Edward VI the Minster was stripped of 67 manors, part of the endowment of the See of York handed over to the King.

With the combined threat from Philip of Spain and Catholic Mary Queen of Scots, an anti-Papist campaign began and in 1570 Catholics in York were obliged to listen to Protestant sermons. 34 died for their convictions.

Unlike many churches York survived the ravages of the Civil War by the influence of Sir Thomas Fairfax, a Cromwellian general and a Yorkshireman.

The roof of the South Transept was destroyed by fire on the 9 July 1984. Restoration of the roof, glass and 62 carved bosses, some designed by children, cost in the region of £2¼ million and the Minster's permanent craftsmen are now involved in a ten year project to restore the worn stonework on the West Front of the cathedral.

Acknowledgments

Dr George Carey, Archbishop of Canterbury
Rev.D. Canon Colin Fletcher, Chaplain to the Archbishop of Canterbury
The Provosts, Deans and Chapters of the Cathedrals
Terence Shand
Eleanor Bentall (Photograph)
Geoffrey Butcher FCSD (Designer)
Michael Tremlett
Caroline Houching
The Cathedral Guides